Modelling Railways Illustrated Handl

An Introduction to Modelling
NARROW GAUGE RAILWAYS

Pete McParlin's Snake River Lumber Co., in HO scale on 9mm gauge track, is set in the backwoods of the United States. (Alan Cook)

By David Cox
(Greenwich & District Narrow Gauge Society)

IRWELL PRESS

Copyright Irwell Press 1995
ISBN 1-871608-45-7

CONTENTS

Chapter 1
INTRODUCTION 1

Chapter 2
SCALES and GAUGES 12

Chapter 3
PROTOTYPES 19

Chapter 4
MODELLING NARROW GAUGE RAILWAYS 26

Chapter 5
TRACK 42

Chapter 6
COUPLINGS 44

Chapter 7
NARROW GAUGE LOCOMOTIVE KITS 48

Chapter 8
NARROW GAUGE LAYOUTS 53

Chapter 9
SOURCES of INFORMATION 68

Acknowledgements 70

Published in the United Kingdom by
IRWELL PRESS,
P.O.Box 1260, Caernarfon,
Gwynedd, LL55 3ZD
Printed and Bound by The Amadeus Press,
Huddersfield, West Yorkshire

Chapter One
INTRODUCTION

Standard and Narrow Gauge compared on Gordon Gravett's 7mm scale Llandydref.

Judging by some of the questions that exhibitors of narrow gauge layouts are frequently asked, a great many people have never even heard of narrow gauge railways. Indeed, the confusion and ill-informed speculation that is often overheard on the other side of the barrier at model railway exhibitions can be a source of both amusement and irritation to the aficionados behind the layout. But there is no reason why most people, particularly those with only a marginal interest in the hobby, should know what narrow gauge is. It is as well, too, that those who do exhibit narrow gauge layouts should treat even the most naive of questions with courtesy. After all, we all have to start somewhere...

The writer of this Handbook assumes that you do at least know what narrow gauge railways are, even if you don't know very much about them. It is intended as an introduction to modelling such lines in the smaller scales, although it is not aimed at the complete newcomer. For this reason, it does not tell you how to build baseboards, lay track, electrify it, construct buildings and scenery and so forth. These topics are common to all model railways, standard and narrow gauge, and information on them can readily be found elsewhere. Rather, this book is about those matters which are specific to the modelling of narrow gauge railways - their appeal, the pitfalls, the problems - and most importantly, the delights of this particularly fascinating branch of the model railway hobby.

What Is Narrow Gauge?
Having firmly stated that I assume you know what narrow gauge railways are, it will doubtless seem perverse to start off with a chapter implying precisely the opposite. However, the term "narrow gauge" can mean an awful lot of different things and it is as well to define just what they are.

Back in the early days of the nineteenth century when the first steam powered railways were pioneered, their builders settled on a gauge (ie, the distance between the parallel rails) of four feet eight and a half inches (or 1,435mm). Quite why this somewhat eccentric measurement was chosen is not known, but as a result, almost all of the major railways in this country (and

A typically large 3 foot 6 inch gauge loco once used on a railway in Zambia. Although technically narrow gauge, 3 foot 6 inch is the standard gauge of many countries throughout the world.

An Introduction to Modelling Narrow Gauge Railways

Passenger carrying narrow gauge railways are major tourist attractions, either preserved or specially built as on the 2 foot gauge line in the Hollycoombe Country Park in Hampshire. The loco is a Barclay E class 0-4-0WT.

most others as well) have track laid to this gauge which is now commonly referred to as "standard gauge". Obviously, any railway with a track gauge less than 1435mm is narrow gauge.

That, at least, is true for this country, although it is worth pointing out that a few others settled on different gauges as their standard. Ireland, India, Russia and Finland, for example, chose gauges which are wider at 5 foot and over, whilst others, such as New Zealand and South Africa, are narrower at 3 foot 6 inches. Pedants would maintain that in the former countries, 1435mm gauge is effectively narrow gauge!

Although the 3 foot 6 inch gauge systems of South Africa, New Zealand and others are, strictly speaking, narrow gauge, this Handbook is not really concerned with them. They are, in effect, the equivalent of our standard gauge railways and as such, have very little in common with what we, in this country, consider to be narrow gauge.

Once upon a time, there were a great many narrow gauge railways in this country and the gauges they employed varied enormously, from as little as 12 inches to as much as 4 foot 6 inches, with a whole range of others in between, some being differentiated by less than an inch. The commonest ones, however, were 15 inch (used mainly, but not wholly, for miniature railways), 18 inch, 2 foot (or thereabouts: 1 foot 10 1/2 inches and 1 foot 11 1/2 inches were also popular), 2 foot 3 inches, 2 foot 6 inches, 3 foot and 3 foot 6 inches. Of course, almost all have now disappeared, only a very few surviving either as a result of certain specialised circumstances in industry or as preserved or tourist lines.

The Appeal of Narrow Gauge Railways

So why do some people choose to model them as opposed to the majority who build miniature replicas of standard gauge railways? The answer lies, for many modellers, in the individuality of the prototypes. The huge diversity of track gauges is but one reflection of their diversity as a whole.

Most enthusiasts tend to choose one or other of the major standard gauge companies to model. As is inevitable with large organisations, there was a strong tendency towards standardisation which extended not simply to just the locos and rolling stock, but also to the stations themselves. Each company tended to build structures in a similar style, paint them the same colours all over their system, equip them with the same kind of seating, fencing, signalling and so on, to such an extent that it is usually possible for the knowledgeable railway enthusiast to recognise which was the original owning company of most stations. This is true even today (always provided, of course, that a station has not been completely flattened and rebuilt), despite the inevitable changes brought about by grouping, nationalisation, modernisation, rationalisation, privatisation and all the other 'isations' that have afflicted our railways.

There were, of course, smaller companies which, by and large, were more individualistic, particularly the light railways, such as the Easingwold, Kent and East Sussex, Bishops Castle and so on. Narrow gauge lines had a great deal in common with these railways, both varieties being very minor concerns. However, the wider gauge companies often used locos and stock purchased second or even third hand from the main line companies or if they didn't, they bought the standard designs of loco manufacturers like Manning Wardle and Hudswell Clarke. On the other hand, the motive power of almost every public passenger and freight carrying narrow gauge railway was, with a mere two exceptions, unique to each particular company. One of those exceptions was pretty odd, too, in that the locomotives concerned were all American built, purchased secondhand from the War Department after the First World War. Only three lines purchased them and two of those had only one each. The other exception was the Ballymena and Larne in Northern Ireland which bought a couple of locos of the same design as those on the Isle of Man Railway, although its other locos formed a very varied collection indeed. Rolling stock, too, both passenger and goods, was also unique to each of the common carriers, whereas freight on the standard gauge minor railways was nearly always handled in wagons belonging to the main line companies.

Narrow gauge railways were constructed to save money, being considerably cheaper to build than standard gauge ones. Smaller locos and stock required only a narrow track bed and were able to traverse much tighter curves. Consequently, track could follow much more closely the contours of the land, so avoiding the need for large and ex-

Only three of the public narrow gauge railways on the mainland of Britain had locomotives of the same design. These were all American locos purchased second-hand from the War Department after the First War. A 4n9 model built by David Woodcock.(D.L.Taylor)

All of the ex-WD Baldwin's used in this country were scrapped long ago, but two which were sold abroad after World War One have been brought back for use on preserved lines. This example worked in a sugar factory in India, but is now undergoing restoration on the Leighton Buzzard Narrow Gauge Railway.

pensive earthworks. The savings thus achieved meant that railways could be built in hilly or mountainous terrain where the cost of laying a standard gauge line was prohibitive or where the level of traffic simply would not justify one.

Inevitably, lines were constructed by overly optimistic promoters in areas with only a very small population and hardly any industry, certainly not enough to support even an inexpensive narrow gauge railway. One or two, notably the Ravenglass and Eskdale, fell into the hands of the Official Receiver fairly soon after they were opened. Many others were built on the cheap and struggled to survive on a 'make do and mend' basis as traffic receipts barely covered running costs and left none for investing in new track, locos or stock. Indeed, on a number of railways there was hardly enough money for even the absolute minimum of maintenance. Fortunately for their Managements, speeds were inevitably slow, so the lack of adequate safety measures rarely resulted in anything more disastrous than the odd derailment or two, which was not, of course, worth reporting to the Authorities....

This, then, is the commonly perceived view of the typical British narrow gauge railway. It is one of small, idiosyncratic locos hauling trains composed of quaint rolling stock of similar proportions, trundling slowly on overgrown track meandering along some forgotten valley that few people have heard of and even fewer visited, between nowhere in particular and somewhere equally unimportant.

But it is by no means a true picture of all narrow gauge lines. The Festiniog was a notable exception and was highly profitable as a result of the huge tonnage of slate it carried down from Blaenau Festiniog to Portmadoc, at least, until the 1930s. Indeed, as the pioneer of steam traction on rails as narrow as 2 foot apart, in the last century, it drew visitors from all over the world, including Europe, the United States and even a representative of the Czar of Russia. The Corris Railway in Mid Wales, too, was quite a prosperous little line, returning a handsome dividend on its shares for a number of years. Other railway companies, despite the lack of potential traffic, were surprisingly well engineered. The Lynton and Barnstaple was one and after it was taken over by the Southern Railway at the grouping in 1923, had a great deal of money invested in it. Alas, it was to no avail as receipts dwindled to the point where the Southern closed it in 1935. Another well equipped line was the wonderfully named Leek and Manifold, which was unique in this country for using transporter wagons to carry standard gauge wagons on its 2 foot 6 inch gauge tracks, thus saving the costs of transhipping freight. Unfortunately, it ran, very efficiently and very economically, from nowhere to nowhere in a particularly beautiful part of Staffordshire and when a dairy near its terminus closed, it started to make a loss. The LMS were then its owners and lost no time in closing it.

Narrow gauge railways, being (obviously) narrower, intruded far less into the landscape than did their wider

The Festiniog Railway pioneered the use of steam power on track as narrow as 2 foot with this type of loco. This view of 'Prince' was taken in the early 1950s shortly after it had been restored to working order by the preservation society. (P E K Morgan/GDNGRS Collection)

An Introduction to Modelling Narrow Gauge Railways

Towards the end of its existence, the Great Western Railway ran only a thrice weekly goods service on the Corris Railway with the remaining two locos. Fortunately, both survived and can now be found on the Talyllyn Railway. This is no. 3 running round its train at Towyn Wharf.

gauge contemporaries. They were very much more part of the countryside, but not simply just in the visual sense. Serving often remote areas well away from the prying eyes of officialdom, their operation was very much more geared to the needs of the scattered communities they served and, not least, to the convenience of those who ran them. Towards the end of its life, the Corris found itself part of the Great Western Railway which stated in its working timetables that goods trains ran on Tuesdays, Thursdays and Saturdays. In fact, they didn't: they ran on Mondays, Wednesdays and Fridays, because this fitted in more with the half day's fishing of the stationmaster at Machynlleth!

It was not uncommon for deliveries to a pub situated close to the line to be made by the train offloading barrels of beer at the nearest level crossing and not at the station where they should have been. At one point, the line threaded its way round the backs of the houses in the village of Corris itself and when coal for domestic use had been ordered, it was quite usual for the train staff to shovel it direct into the backyards, rather than haul it to the station and then have to go to the trouble of carting it all the way back again. On occasions, wagons were simply derailed and then run down the road to unload, a relatively easy task given the small size of the Corris's rolling stock. No doubt the Great Western's Management would have thrown a fit or two had they known, but Paddington was two hundred miles away and what they didn't know, couldn't hurt them.

By the late 1920s and early 1930s, virtually all the narrow gauge companies were struggling and most, even those not built on the cheap, looked run down and often rather clapped out as competition from buses and lorries began to be felt and as the economic slump hit almost all areas of the country. Dilapidation, whilst not necessarily very appealing when full size, can be very attractive in model form. Rusting corrugated iron and rotting timber buildings surrounded by piles of discarded or broken equipment can, when modelled properly and with skill, give a layout great character and realism.

The above description does not really apply to those narrow gauge railways which still exist (although it must be admitted that quite a few enthusiast-run lines do seem to have an excessive amount of what is apparently "junk" lying around). Those that managed to survive to be preserved have only done

"... The locos were small and idiosyncratic in appearance...." A Kerr Stuart Wren class 0-4-0 built for industrial use, but now privately preserved.

"Narrow gauge trains wandered slowly on overgrown track ..." Towyn Pendre in the early 1950s not long after the Preservation Society took over the Talyllyn. Some of the track in this view would be almost impossible to model. (P E K Morgan/GDNGRS Collection)

so by transforming themselves into tourist attractions and have inevitably changed a great deal in the process. Some, those few who knew them before they were preserved, would argue that they have lost much of their charm and character as a result, but most of us were born too late to know them in their original state. We must at least be thankful that they still exist and that we can capture at least some of their flavour.

The Advantages Of Modelling Narrow Gauge Railways...

There are of course a number of practical advantages to modelling narrow gauge railways, the most obvious one being that of space. Trains were shorter and the stock often considerably smaller than standard gauge ones. A Talyllyn Railway train in the pre preservation period, for example, consisting of one of its two original locos, all four coaches and the brakevan (which was almost invariably attached to all passenger trains) measures a mere 16 inches in 4mm scale and only 29 in 7mm scale. On the other hand, the heaviest train allowed on the Lynton and Barnstaple Railway, nine bogie vehicles double headed by two locos, comes out at almost 5 feet in 4mm scale. This is quite a lot, but by comparison, a standard gauge express with a similar number of coaches and, say, a 4-6-0, would occupy something between eight and a half and nine feet. However, double headed nine coach trains were pretty rare on the L & B, usually being confined to only a very few services during the summer. Outside of the holiday period, trains often consisted of a couple of coaches, which with an engine, is less than 18 inches overall.

The ability of narrow gauge stock to go round tighter curves, particularly those intended for industrial use, is a real space saver. Some of the smaller locos could cope with radii which even in 7mm scale can be measured in inches rather than feet. In 4mm scale, a 15 inch radius curve is very close to the limit of what standard gauge stock can cope with and moreover, it looks faintly ridiculous whilst going round them. With narrow gauge in this scale, 15 inches is

The ability of narrow gauge stock to go round tighter curves, particularly those intended for industrial use, is well illustrated by this view of the peat carrying line owned by Middlebrook Mushrooms Ltd. (D A Brewer)

The choice of a larger scale, such as 7mm, is a much more practical proposition with narrow gauge. These two models of identical locos - both small cabless Hunslets built by Pete Wilson - illustrate the difference between 4mm and 7mm.

An Introduction to Modelling Narrow Gauge Railways

Exploiting the ability of industrial locos and stock to cope with 3 - 4 inch radius curves, Adit 2 in 7mm scale occupies a space less than 2 foot long by 18 inches. (Roy C Link)

quite generous and trains negotiating them appear realistic.

Stations, too, were simpler and occupied less space than their standard gauge equivalents. The Greenwich and District Narrow Gauge Railway Society's exact scale model of Towyn Wharf on the Talyllyn Railway in 4mm scale, for example, is only 4 foot 7 inches long by 2 foot 6 inches at its widest point.

All of this means that more can be fitted in a given space than is feasible with standard gauge. With a conventional terminus to hidden sidings type of set-up, rather than reproducing just one station, it might be possible to include an additional one so that trains can be crossed. If length is a problem, rather than opt for a straight run from one end of the layout to the other, the track can be turned through 180 degrees without any major loss of realism, on baseboards which are only a little wider than the norm. This would allow room for a second station on the other side of the baseboard, although it would be advisable for the scenery to be arranged into 'view blocks' so that it is impossible to see one station from the other.

It is also not wholly impractical to model an entire narrow gauge railway, whereas it is way beyond the scope of the average modeller to reproduce a complete standard gauge line, even a simple branch. By careful selection of prototype and with some judicious compression, one could build the major stations and salient features of one of the simpler lines in, say, a small box room.

However, the temptation to cram as much track as possible into whatever area you have available should be resisted, or at least, thought through very carefully. The prototypes were essentially simple and by stuffing that famous quart into the proverbial pint pot, a great deal of the character and appeal of the real thing will be lost. A more realistic alternative would be to devote more space to scenic development. In recent years, the 'railway in a landscape' approach has become much more prevalent, largely due to the influence of Barry Norman, whose magnificent layout 'Petherick' has been widely seen both in the model press and at exhibitions. Few modellers can afford 4 or 5 foot wide baseboards, but the narrow trackbed and simple stations of narrow gauge railways readily lend themselves to being "lost" amongst miniature hillsides and fields on baseboards of only average width.

The choice of a larger scale, such as 7mm, is a much more realistic proposition with narrow gauge. There are a few standard gauge layouts in this scale which occupy a very small space, but they tend to be models of only bits of stations and are often so simple as to have virtually no operating interest at all. A reasonably complete 7mm narrow gauge station with all the usual features, on the other hand, can be built in an area no greater than the average 4mm scale standard gauge branch line. 7mm narrow gauge kits are also noticeably cheaper than those for standard gauge (by up to about 50% in some instances) and there is no real discernible difference in quality either.

Those who model in 7mm scale (and I am one of them and therefore undoubtedly biased, having changed from 4mm a few years ago!) claim a number of advantages. Obviously, being bigger, it is easier to see and incorporate more detail, but the increased bulk and weight of the models gives them a greater feel of the prototypes. They tend to move much more like the real thing, grinding around curves and dipping and lurching over rail joints in a very realistic manner. Operation, too, is often a little more reliable than in the smaller scales.

A number of modellers are unfortunate enough to have almost no space available at all in which to build a layout. Yet even those who live in bedsits or very crowded circumstances can construct a worthwhile narrow gauge model in a tiny area. Pagham Harbour is built on two baseboards occupying a total area 5 foot 4 inches by 16 inches. Interestingly, its constructor, Richard Glover, started it not because of lack of space but rather lack of time.

But even Pagham Harbour is large when compared with some layouts. David Barham's Adit 2 is actually a 7mm scale model, yet is less than 2 foot long and 18 inches wide. Exploiting the ability of industrial locos and stock to cope with extremely tight curves (in this case of 3 - 4 inches radius), it represents a temporary 2 foot gauge railway laid down by a contractor to remove rock and earth from a tunnelling project and to deliver supplies and equipment. The gauge of the track is exact scale (14mm) and its configuration, even those 3 inch radius curves, is accurate, being based on steel sleepered portable track produced by the Leeds based railway suppliers, Robert Hudson Ltd., who are still in business today.

Finally, mention must be made of the 'rabbit warren' type of layout, although it must be admitted that there seem to be very few of them about these days. A rabbit warren is the antithesis of the 'railway in a landscape' model, because quarts, and sometimes, even gallons, are stuffed into pint pots. Basically, these

A considerable number of narrow gauge railways abroad made extensive use of railcars, but none ever tried them in mainland Britain. However, some of the 3 foot gauge lines in both Northern Ireland and Eire did, notably the County Donegal Railways. This is a 4mm scale model of its No.14, constructed from a Backwoods Miniatures kit. (Alan Cook)

Modelling Railways Illustrated Handbook No.5

Narrow gauge railways, with their simple stations and much slimmer trackbeds, make it much easier to adopt the 'railway in a landscape' approach. This is Barry Jeffery's 'Lindal End' layout in 4n9. (George Ansell)

Towyn Wharf on the Talyllyn Railway can be fitted into an area 4 foot 7 inches by 2 foot 6 inches in 4mm scale. This is the Greenwich & District Narrow Gauge Society's version.

layouts have track with exceptionally tight curves and gradients, which winds around, over and under itself and pops in and out of tunnels - hence, the term 'rabbit warren'. At one time, they were very popular, almost every narrow gauge layout that was exhibited being of this type.

Some real railways traversing mountainous territory adopt loops and spirals to gain height, notably the Darjeeling line in India and some of those situated in the Alps. Nearer to home, the Festiniog climbs over itself at Dduallt. The existence of such real situations is often used as a prototypical justification for rabbit warrens, but quite frankly, this is really rather spurious as they bear very little resemblance to what full size railways do in such circumstances. For this reason, serious narrow gauge modellers tended to denigrate them to such an extent that one hardly sees them these days. However, as a genre of narrow gauge modelling, they can be quite fun to build and look at and if you want to build one, no one is stopping you, but they are not really very railway-like.

...And The Disadvantages

For the enthusiast who has been sold on narrow gauge, there are none! The appeal of the prototypes is enough to overcome whatever problems may be encountered. However, this book is intended as an introduction to narrow gauge modelling and for someone new to this particular branch of the hobby, it is as well to be aware of the differences between narrow and standard gauge modelling.

Firstly, it is no use going to your local toy shop expecting to purchase a ready to run narrow gauge train set. There are such sets available, but they

Ready to run locos in HO scale for use on 9mm gauge track produced the French firm, Jouef. Although based on narrow gauge prototypes from Germany, their dimensions have been significantly altered.

An Introduction to Modelling Narrow Gauge Railways

Roco of Austria also manufacture ready to run HO scale narrow gauge stock. This is their steam loco, a small 0-6-0T of freelance design.

are produced by European manufacturers and, not surprisingly, are models of overseas prototypes. If you want to model the British narrow gauge scene realistically, then you are going to have to tackle kits.

Whilst this may be daunting if you have never done it before, there are several which are very easy to construct and eminently suitable for the beginner. Many of the more recently produced plastic kits for wagons and coaches, by such firms as Meridian Models and Parkside Dundas in 4mm scale are very simple, whilst some loco kits in this scale are only a little more complicated - but not necessarily more difficult. Almost all are designed to fit onto commercial N gauge chassis, some with very little modification indeed. Whilst a few loco kits in 7mm scale are intended to utilise commercial 00 chassis, they do tend to be a little more difficult, as do some of the rolling stock kits. Nevertheless, some can quite readily be tackled by a beginner provided they have a little patience and is prepared to take care.

Roco also produce a 6 wheel diesel. This, too is freelance.

Ready to run stock in 7mm scale is produced by Fleischmann under their 'Magic Train' label, the prototypes of which are Austrian. The loco comes with either simplified or fully detailed valve gear. This is the fully detailed version.

Having implied that such ready to run models as are available are unsuitable for the British scene, it is worth pointing out that several European built locos did, and indeed still, operate in this country. Several preserved narrow gauge railways have them, notably the Welshpool and Llanfair which not only has a German built 0-8-0 imported from Austria, but also some 4 wheel coaches from the Zillertalbahn, along with a large 2-6-2 from Finland. The W & L is by no means alone: the Brecon Mountains, Leighton Buzzard, South Tynedale and Amberley Chalk Pits Museum, amongst others, also have motive power from overseas. This is not a recent phenomenon either. The German firm, Orenstein & Koppel (still in the railway business, but nowadays better known as escalator manufacturers) sold some 30 to 40 steam locos in this country before the First World War, all of them to industry, and a fair number

The Welshpool and Llanfair Preservation Society imported this German built 0-8-0T from Austria.

An Introduction to Modelling Narrow Gauge Railways

The Brecon Mountains Railway runs trains with an 0-6-2 purchased from the former East German State Railway.

of internal combustion ones between the two Wars. Then, there were the American built machines which were purchased by the War Department during the 1914-18 War and which were subsequently sold to several British railway companies.

However, it is as well to mention that none of the prototypes of the RTR narrow gauge models produced abroad ever ran in this country. Almost all are also built to different scales, too. HO has a prototype to model ratio of 1:87 rather than the 1:76 of 4mm (or 00), whilst European 0 is 1:45 rather than 1:43.5 in this country). As will be apparent, the differences are minimal, so if you have never tackled a kit before, it might be worthwhile obtaining one so that you can at least get something running.

Alternatively, you could choose to reproduce one of the many European narrow gauge railways of which there are some fascinating and very modellable ones. Most of the RTR models are of German or Austrian prototypes, although there is a very considerable range covering the electrified metre gauge lines of Switzerland. In order to produce a convincing model, however, some research will be necessary as narrow gauge railways in Europe are very different to those in the UK in the way that track and stations are laid out, methods of operation and the equipment used. One advantage is that in Europe,

Before the First World War, the German company of Orenstein and Koppel sold a number of engines in this country, including this one, which was purchased by a contractor. It was eventually acquired by the Penrhyn Slate Quarry where it was photographed 'dumped' in the 1950s. (P E K Morgan/GDNGRS Collection)

notably in Austria and what was formerly East Germany, a number still survive as working (as opposed to preserved) lines.

RTR models of American locos and stock can also be found, but they tend, on the whole, to be highly detailed and rather expensive brass models produced usually in Far East. Many are intended only as showcase models and consequently need a certain amount of work to persuade them to run properly. Again, if you choose to set your layout in the United States, you will need to find out what the prototypes were like as railway practice on the other side of the Atlantic is not the same as that in this country.

And the other disadvantages of narrow gauge modelling? The main one, it must be said, is that the operation of narrow gauge railways was not particularly complex. If you enjoy the kind of intensive service that you get from running a model of Clapham Junction or Crewe, then narrow gauge is not for you. Many prototypes only ran two or three trains a day and usually on a one engine in steam basis, whilst those with a more frequent service rarely had more than eight or so trains a day at the outside.

Some industrial railways were rather busier, however. During its heyday, the extensive 18 inch gauge system at the Woolwich Arsenal in South East London (which manufactured munitions and handled other supplies for the military) ran a half hourly passenger service for the benefit of its workmen as well as transporting many thousands of tons of material round the site. A little further eastwards along the Thames is the 2 foot 6 inch gauge Sittingbourne and Kemsley Light Railway. Although now preserved and carrying passengers only, it was originally built to connect a wharf with several paper mills. A great deal of freight was carried and, at one time, a round the clock, 24 hour passenger service also existed for the benefit of shiftworkers.

Wholly industrial lines do not appeal to everyone. Very often, their surroundings were fairly grim and unattractive, to say the least. Those who prefer to model a more traditionally bucolic, common carrier type railway can still find a lot to interest them operationally, although it will be much gentler and rather less frenzied than running Clapham Junction.

One thing that distinguishes narrow gauge railways from most (but by no means all) standard gauge lines which does significantly increase their operational interest is the mixed train. In order to keep costs low, very few (if any) narrow gauge lines in this country ran separate freight trains, simply tacking goods wagons on to the ends of some of their regular passenger services as and when required. From the modeller's point of view, shunting is the most interesting and varied aspect of running trains and the mixed provides ample scope for lots of enjoyable shuffling of vehicles.

The normal pattern of operations was for lightly loaded services to be mixed with usually only a single coach, whilst the more heavily frequented passenger services would be strengthened with as many additional coaches as necessary or were available. Thus, not only can one shunt wagons around, but one can also shuffle coaches, too.

Above left: Industrial lines were usually situated in grim and unattractive surroundings, but those built for agricultural and forestry use were an exception. The Drefor Tramway is a 4mm scale model of a Timber carrying railway.

Below: The classic narrow gauge mixed passenger and goods train in model form. A scene on David Taylor's Charmouth layout in 7mm scale. (D L Taylor)

Chapter Two
SCALES and GAUGES

A scratchbuilt model of the Kerry Tramway's unique Bagnall 0-4-2 inverted saddle tank, 'Excelsior', on the 7N16.5 Pentre Tramway.

The terms 'scale' and 'gauge' are often the cause of much confusion, largely because they tend to be used indiscriminately. For the purposes of this book, 'gauge' is the distance between the rails and 'scale' is the proportion or ratio between a model and its full size prototype. Thus, a model in the most common scale (00) is 76 times smaller than the real thing. Scale need not always be expressed as a ratio: in 1:76 scale, 4mm represents 1 foot.

The nomenclature for the scales and gauges used when modelling narrow gauge railways is even more confusing, not least because several different systems of terminology are currently in use. For instance, modelling in 4mm scale using a track gauge of 9mm is described variously as 00n2¼, 009 and 4n9. Its very close cousin, 3.5mm scale (or HO) is known as HOn 2½, HO9, 3.5n9 or HOe!

One system of terminology, perhaps the oldest, uses the scale of the model, followed by 'n' to indicate narrow gauge, followed by the gauge of the prototype. Thus, 00 = scale, n = narrow gauge, 2¼ = 2¼ feet or 2 foot 3 inches. Another system omits the 'n' altogether, using merely the scale (00) followed by the model gauge used: hence 009 and 016.5.

There are several illogicalities in both these systems, not least of which is that 00 is often used by standard gauge modellers to describe a gauge, not a scale. Another problem is that the model gauges in use sometimes have no prototype equivalent, the most obvious example being HO9. In Europe, the problem seems to have been solved by using only two suffixes after the scale, 'm' for models representing metre gauge prototypes and 'e' for anything less than

The most popular narrow gauge scale is 4n9, more commonly known as 009, for which a great many loco and rolling stock kits are available. A scene on David Gander's Nantgwyn with a Chivers Finelines Kerr Stuart 'Skylark' class on the right and a Saltford Models de Winton vertical boilered loco on the left, along with a variety of wagons built from plastic kits. (David Gander)

Another whitemetal loco kit for 4n9, this one being produced by Roxey Mouldings. The prototype is a small Kerr Stuart built for the Metropolitan Water Board in London.

they choose to model in. Using an established scale and an established gauge makes life a lot easier because there is a great deal more trade support than there would be by inventing one's own scale/gauge combination. In 4mm and 7mm scales, for example, such things as figures, scenic accessories, fencing and the like are readily available as well as a number of kits of narrow gauge prototypes.

Similarly, using the gauge of one of the more common scales gives one access to a whole range of commercial chassis, wheels, motors and other mechanical components. For this reason, 7mm scale modellers tend to use the same gauge track as 4mm standard gauge (16.5), whilst 4mm scale modellers use N gauge (9mm).

There are a number of modellers who use an uncommon scale/gauge combination, but they do end up having to scratchbuild a great deal as a result. For instance, some people use 16.5mm gauge track with a scale of 8mm to the foot to represent 2 foot gauge prototypes

A small 0-6-0T from Chivers Finelines on a Roco chassis shunts at Chris Krupas 4n9 minimum space layout, Minbury Abbas. The prototype was built to a design of the French firm, Decauville, by Kerr Stuart of Stoke On Trent during the First World War.

that. The most common scale/gauge combinations are H0m for models in HO scale on 12mm gauge track and HOe for models on 9mm gauge track, although a recent development is HOg (or HOf and HOz!) for models on Z (6.5mm) gauge track. 0m and 0e are the 0 scale equivalents.

Perhaps the most sensible and logical system of terminology is to use the scale of the model expressed as a figure (i.e., as the number of millimetres to the foot), followed by 'n' (to indicate narrow gauge), followed by the model gauge in use. Thus, 009 becomes 4n9, HO9 is 3.5n9, 016.5 is 7n16.5 and so on. This is the system adopted for the purposes of this book, although in the review of scale/gauge combinations that follows, as many other terms for the same thing as are known to the author will be given.

Naturally, any scale/gauge combination can be employed, but generally, narrow gauge modellers use track gauges which are the standard gauges of a scale or two smaller than the one more accurately. Whilst they are able to use 4mm scale wheels, motors and gears, there are no miniature people or scenic accessories available in 8mm to the foot. For the newcomer to narrow gauge, it makes much more sense to stick to one of the established scales and gauges.

Scales and Gauges in 4mm Scale
4n9 (00n2¼, but most commonly 009) is undoubtedly the most popular of the narrow gauge scales using 4mm scale

An Introduction to Modelling Narrow Gauge Railways

The wonderfully eccentric Irish 3 foot gauge lines can be modelled in 4n12 or 7n21. This is the County Donegal Railways 'Columbkille', a large 2-6-4T. (P E K Morgan/GDNGRS Collection)

on the same gauge track as N gauge. This accurately represents 2 foot 3 inch gauge and is consequently ideal for modelling the Talyllyn, the Corris and the Campbelltown and Macrihanish, but it is also frequently used to represent gauges between 2 foot and 2 foot 6 inches.

4n12 (0012, 00n3) used to be the most common scale/gauge before the advent of 4n9, employing 4mm scale with 12mm wide TT track. Up to the early 1960s, Triang (now Hornby) used to produce a ready to run range of TT (or 3mm to the foot) standard gauge models and most narrow gauge modellers used to scratchbuild bodies on their loco chassis, bogies and wheels. The arrival of N gauge meant the demise of commercial TT equipment (at least in this country) and with it, the rise of 4n9. This was a pity as 12mm track in 4mm scale gives an exact gauge for 3 foot gauge prototypes such as the Isle of Man Railways, the Southwold Railway and all of the wonderfully eccentric Irish lines. Indeed, a few whitemetal kits were produced in the 1960s, but after three decades of virtual extinction, there seems to be a resurgence of interest in 4n12,

A kit for 'Columbkille' in 4n12 is available from Backwoods Miniatures. (Alan Cook)

Modelling Railways Illustrated Handbook No.5

Another Irish 3 foot gauge line which can be readily reproduced in 4n12 using kits is the Clogher Valley. This is the Backwoods Miniatures kit for one of the line's original locomotives. Branchlines produce kits of some of the coaches. (Alan Cook)

with several manufacturers entering the field.

4n8 gives an accurate 2 foot gauge in 4mm scale with 8mm gauge trackwork. Obviously, most 4n9 kits can be used, but whilst N gauge wheels can, in some instances, be readily pushed in by 1mm on their axles, chassis for locomotives usually have to be scratchbuilt.

4n6.5 uses Z gauge (6.5mm) track with 4mm scale to produce models of 18 inch gauge. The first person to use and exhibit a layout with this scale/gauge combination was Greenwich & District Narrow Gauge Society member, Christopher Krupa, who christened it Z4, by which it is also known!

Scales and Gauges in 7mm Scale

7n16.5 (0 16.5) is the most common of the larger scales, using 00 gauge track (16.5) with a ratio of 1:43.5. This gives a scale gauge of 2 foot 4 1/4 inches and is therefore suitable for models of the Glyn Valley Tramway and a very few industrial railways such as the Snailbeach in Shropshire and the Threlkeld Quarry line in the Lake District. In practice, modellers use it for a range of prototypes of other gauges, from 2 foot to 2 foot 6 inches, just as they do 4n9. There was, in fact, one well known layout on the exhibition circuit which used 16.5mm gauge to represent an imaginary Irish 3 foot gauge line, even though it was 4.5mm too narrow.

4n12 is enjoying something of a renaissance with several manufacturers producing kits for this scale/gauge combination. These are models of Tralee & Dingle prototypes made by Branchlines.

15

An Introduction to Modelling Narrow Gauge Railways

This Wrightlines Fowler Marshall diesel in 7mm scale comes with its own, easy to assemble chassis. It can be made to either 14mm or 16.5mm gauges.

A small number of kits in 7n21 are now becoming available, such as this Clogher Valley coach, one of two types for this railway produced by Branchlines. They can also be built to 16.5mm gauge and 4mm scale versions are also on sale.

Modelling 2 foot gauge accurately in 7mm scale is now easier for the beginner, largely due to Roy C Link who produced the first 14mm gauge loco kit, a Ruston LAT shown here.

The result was nevertheless quite successful.

7n14 uses 14mm gauge track to accurately portray 2 foot gauge prototypes. There is some trade support, largely pioneered by Roy C Link with his growing range of high quality loco and rolling stock kits, although at the time of writing, these are restricted to industrial prototypes. Obviously, the loco kits come with their own chassis, but in order to make it easy for the beginner, they are usually ready assembled or virtually so. Track components are also available, along with various jigs, templates and the like, as well as a great deal of information about both modelling and prototype matters.

Interest in 7n14 appears to be growing as one of the other major kit producers in 7mm scale, Wrightlines, intends that all of their future kits (where appropriate) will be capable of being constructed to 14mm gauge as well as 16.5mm gauge.

7n9 involves 7mm scale on 9mm or N gauge track. There are some kits in this scale/gauge combination of 18 inch gauge prototypes, which are a little undergauged, 9mm being as near 15 inches as to make no difference. As such, it is ideal for those interested in modelling miniature railways such as the Ravenglass and Eskdale and the Romney, Hythe and Dymchurch.

7n6.5 uses Z gauge track to represent even smaller miniature railway gauges, such as 10 1/4 inch. Christopher Krupa also pioneered this combination, too!

Scratchbuilder Scales

As mentioned above, almost any scale/gauge combination can be utilised provided you are prepared to scratchbuild. Some, but by no means all, combinations which have been employed by modellers in the past are listed here:

3n9 (TTn3, TT9) 3mm to the foot scale on 9mm gauge track to represent 3 foot gauge prototypes.

Above and below : Roy C Link's beautiful little Crowsnest Tramway was constructed to 1:32 scale (or 3/8 inch to the foot) for which all the railway components had to be scratchbuilt. However, Roy was able to make use of the extensive range of figures, animals, road vehicles etc in this scale which are available mostly for military modellers. (Both Roy C Link)

2n6.5 (Nn3, Nm) N scale on Z gauge track, again representing 3 foot gauge prototypes. There is some, albeit very limited, trade support in Europe and the United States.

5.5n12 uses TT gauge track to represent a prototype gauge of 2 foot. In the 1960s, Gem used to market whitemetal kits of some Talyllyn and Festiniog models for this scale/gauge.

5.5n16.5 allows 3 foot gauge to be modelled using 00 gauge track.

7n21 Another scale/gauge combination which allows the accurate modelling of 3 foot gauge railways using 7mm scale. Pretty rare at the moment, although a couple of manufacturers have produced coach kits for this scale.

8n16.5 A more accurate scale/gauge for 2 foot gauge prototypes than 7n16.5

Common Scales and Gauges in Europe...

H0e (HO9) is the European equivalent of 009. Although the gauge is the same, the scale is different at 3.5mm to the foot with a prototype to model ratio of 1:87. This gives a scale gauge of 783mm or about 2 foot 6 inches. There are quite a few ready to run models and kits available, mostly from Germany and Austria which obviously represent prototypes from those countries.

There were only a very few railways abroad built to 785mm gauge (mainly in Germany), but modellers use H0e to represent quite a wide spread of gauges, from 600mm to 760mm. The former was quite common in France and could also be found in Germany, although 750mm gauge was more frequently employed.

French kits of 600mm gauge prototypes, however, are usually to British 4mm scale, not HOe, as this gives a more accurate scale gauge. 760mm gauge was the standard narrow gauge of the former Austro Hungarian Empire and so was used in all of those countries.

H0m is the European equivalent of 4n12, in this instance representing metre gauge track in 1:87 scale. Unlike 4n12 in this country, H0m has been much more popular because several RTR ranges have been available for quite some time. Bemo initially produced models of German prototypes before embarking on its well known range of models of the electrified lines of Switzerland. More recently, Zeuke have re-entered the H0m field with models of prototypes from what used to be East Germany.

HOg utilises HO scale models on Z gauge track to give a closer to scale gauge for 600mm gauge prototypes.

An Introduction to Modelling Narrow Gauge Railways

Left: HOe or 3.5n9 is the equivalent of 4n9 in Europe. A scene on a layout the author built many years ago which closely followed Austrian practice.

Middle: An unpainted brass model by Sango in 3.5n9 of a prototype used on the Sandy River and Rangeley Lakes Railroad, an extensive 2 foot gauge line which once existed in Maine in the USA.

...and in the United States

HOn3 is the most popular scale/gauge combination in the United States, representing 3 foot gauge on 10.5mm gauge track in 1:87. HOn30 (or HOn2 1/2) is also not uncommon and is exactly the same as HOe in Europe.

S gauge has always had a larger following on the other side of the Atlantic than in this country and Europe and Sn3 is quite well established. Its narrower equivalent, Sn2, on 10.5mm gauge track, is rare but does have its adherents. Ratio is 1:64 or three sixteenths of an inch to a foot.

0n3 and 0n30 (or On21/2) use track gauges of 19mm and 16.5mm respectively, although it is worth pointing out that American 0 scale has a ratio of 1:48, not 1:43.5, as in this country.

What Wales is to British narrow gauge enthusiasts, Colorado is to their American counterparts. This is a Denver and Rio Grande 3 foot gauge loco now on the Cumbres and Toltec Scenic Railroad. Brass models of almost all of the D & RGRR's locos are available in HOn3, Sn3 and 0n3.

Chapter Three
PROTOTYPES

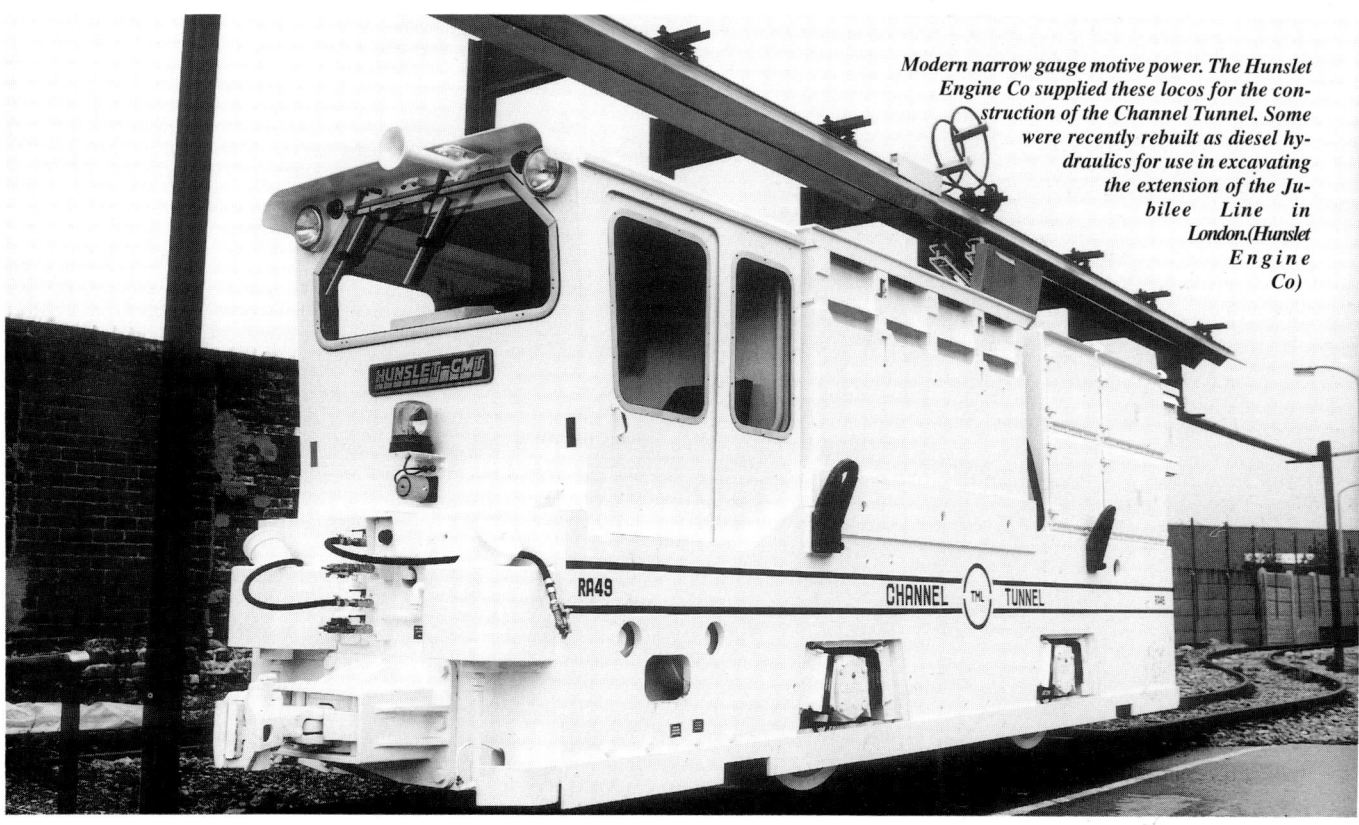

Modern narrow gauge motive power. The Hunslet Engine Co supplied these locos for the construction of the Channel Tunnel. Some were recently rebuilt as diesel hydraulics for use in excavating the extension of the Jubilee Line in London.(Hunslet Engine Co)

Despite the huge diversity of prototype narrow gauge railways, they can be broadly categorised into one of five kinds.

Industrial Railways
The very first railways of all were, in fact, industrial narrow gauge ones. Back in the 15th century, crude railways using manpower and track constructed from timber were in use in mines in what are now Germany, Austria and Hungary. By the 17th century, there were examples of flanged wheels in this country. Since then, particularly after the development of steam power, narrow gauge railways (sometimes called tramways) have been used in almost every manufacturing process throughout the world. The Woolwich Arsenal and the Sittingbourne and Kemsley have already been mentioned, but breweries, chemical works, engineering firms, construction companies, oil refineries, farming and forestry have all utilised them at some time or other. The widest use they have found, however, has been in quarrying and mining.

These days, of course, dump trucks, tracked vehicles, conveyor belts and the like have supplanted them, but there are still a number of situations where they have a significant advantage over other forms of transport. Before the decline of the coal industry, British Coal had extensive systems of narrow gauge lines, both above and below ground, and some private mines still retain them. They are frequently used in tunnelling projects, the most notable example being the Channel Tunnel, and also the underground extension of the Docklands Light Railway from the East End to Bank in the centre of the City of London.

In certain industries, it is impossible to use road vehicles because they are far too heavy (such as in the extraction of peat) and here, very lightly laid narrow gauge lines can still be found. They have also survived in the brick making industry, hauling clay from the fields to the processing plants. One could also, until very recently, find them in the very uncongenial surroundings of a couple of sewage works.

Industrial narrow gauge railways have a great deal to offer the modeller. Usually, but by no means always, their surroundings were fairly grim, but what is unattractive in real life can often make very atmospheric and unusual models. The huge gouges in the moun-

To model an industrial railway effectively, research into the processes involved is necessary in order to understand how the railway fits into it. Photos such as this are invaluable as they show some of the equipment used and give some indication of the layout of the track. This is a sand quarry near Leighton Buzzard.

An Introduction to Modelling Narrow Gauge Railways

A line up of 4n8 locos scratchbuilt by Peter Wilson for his slate quarry layout.

ballast, hardcore (again for roads or construction purposes) or for tarmac, in which case, it would be taken to a tar making plant. All these finished products would then have to be taken to a transhipment point (a road, harbour or standard gauge main line) where they would be transferred for final delivery.

From the operating aspect, the section of the rail network between the various processing plants and the transhipment point offers the most potential. The line inside the quarry itself, running between the rock face and the crushers, screens etc., would have only a very simple shuttle service, whereas the rest of the route can be much more interesting. Not only would wagons containing various sizes of stone have to be shunted, but there would also be a whole range of supplies for the quarry to be transported inwards: coal for power, timber for pit props, buildings, wagon repairs and the like, rail, oil, water, explosives and so on. Even workmens' trains could be run.

Although a large part of the appeal of narrow gauge railways is their distinctiveness, it is true that this does not always apply to industrial lines. Locomotives, by and large, were the standard designs of the various manufacturers bought 'off the shelf'. Hence Bagnall 0-4-0 saddle tanks could be found in slate and granite quarries, on timber tramways, in cable manufacturing works and the like all over the country, whilst their Hunslet equivalents were particularly widespread in the slate industry.

ries), although there are several books on the subject and such organisations as the Industrial Railway and Narrow Gauge Railway Societies often possess useful material.

Research will also enable the modeller to discover which are the most interesting to reproduce. For example, the quarrying of stone (limestone, granite etc.) where narrow gauge railways were particularly common, was usually dealt with in two stages. Firstly, the rock face was broken down into large lumps (normally by explosives) and then transported by narrow gauge line to a processing plant of some kind. This would usu-

tains of North Wales that were the Penrhyn and Dinorwic Slate Quarries are bare, desolate, and windswept, but a number of very good and fascinating layouts of railways serving such places have been constructed.

Quite a few were located, at least in part, in rather more picturesque environments. Both Dinorwic and Penrhyn had lengthy main lines connecting the quarries with ports where the slate was shipped from and these ran through some very attractive countryside.

It is on industrial lines that the track curved most tightly and clearances were most restricted, which means that even the most space-starved modeller can build a layout of one. David Barham's tiny 7mm scale Adit 2 has already been mentioned, but it is by no means the only one.

To build a realistic model of an industrial line, however, a fair amount of research is necessary, not just into the railway itself, but into the various processes of the particular industry concerned and how the railway fitted into them. Information can be difficult to come by (except possibly for slate quar-

These two photos (middle and above) illustrate how the same loco kit can be finished differently. Both are of standard 0-4-0 saddle tanks produced by W G Bagnall: one is as supplied with a pillar cab, whilst the other has had a more extensive one fitted. The kits, incidentally, are the original 7mm scale ones produced by Roy C Link, but now sold in a modified form by Wrightlines.

ally consist of a crusher (or a series of crushers) which would break down the rock into smaller pieces, and a screening plant, which separated the stone into different sizes. Up to about the 1920s, some would be delivered to a shed where setts were made for use on roads. Other stone would be for use as railway

Even if an industrial system did start off with a fairly standardised loco stud, modifications, usually carried out in the company's own workshops, soon added a degree of individuality. Many such locos were often supplied with inadequate protection for the driver and fireman, usually only a pillar cab or a rather

Modelling Railways Illustrated Handbook No.5

On many railways, clearances were very restricted so that loco cabs were often omitted altogether. Hunslet 0-4-0ST 'Covercoat' in the Dinorwic Slate Quarry. (P E K Morgan/GDNGRS Collection)

The slate quarries of North Wales are bare, desolate, windswept places, but have inspired a number of very good and fascinating layouts, notably Pete Wilson's Chwarel Cwm Bach in 4n8.(Roy C Link)

were often omitted altogether, the crew having to remember to duck down when passing through a low tunnel or bridge or under screens or crushers. In rain or snow, conditions must have been very unpleasant, the crews having to wear several layers of clothing to survive. Elsewhere, some loco manufacturers did produce variations of their standard designs with dropped footplates and heavily cut down cabs.

But this is not to say that there were not some industrial lines which did not have locos of a design unique to them. There was the tiny Kerry Tramway in Mid Wales which, when it was first built, had but a single locomotive, a Bagnall 0-4-2 inverted saddle tank named 'Excelsior', the only one of its kind. The Furzebrook Tramway's 'Secundus' is a strange beast constructed by the firm of Bellis and Seeking. The lines laid by potato growers in the Lincolnshire fens also had some very quaint motive power, including one or two which were homebuilt.

Nevertheless, even those railways which used standard designs of motive power still retained a great deal of character, usually much more than similar standard gauge lines. Their small locos, bearing the scars of a tough existence, with dented buffer beams, patches on their tanks, plating fitted to the cabs, toolboxes and sandboxes adorning their footplates, were highly distinctive.

But character does not always come from steam locos. Those lines which relied on internal combustion power, utilising the everyday machines mass produced by Motor Rail, Ruston and Hornsby, Hudson Hunslet, Hudswell Clarke, Fowler and others, could lay claim to a certain distinction. The industry they were employed in, the stock they hauled and the environment in which they worked all provide a great deal of inspiration for modellers.

Mineral And Passenger Railways

This group of railways is really a development of industrial lines in that their primary purpose was to transport minerals (mostly slate), but as they also carried passengers and general freight,

skimpy weatherboard. In areas where clearances allowed, more substantial cabs were often built.

Life on a lot of railways was hard and usually accident prone. Bulldozers, excavators, earthmovers and such like are these days treated in a similar fashion. Their predecessors, narrow gauge locos and wagons, were, after all, only industrial plant and were regarded in exactly the same way. After being damaged, fairly crude repairs were sometimes carried out, resulting in a major change of appearance in the locos concerned. As they grew older, bits from other defunct locos sometimes replaced worn out parts. The 2 foot 8 1/2 inch gauge Furzebrook Tramway in Dorset (which was used to extract china clay) had a Manning Wardle 0-6-0 saddle tank (called 'Tertius') with a failed boiler. It was replaced by one off a loco from a recently re-gauged 3 foot 9 inch gauge line that also belonged to the company. This was too wide to fit in the normal position between the frames and the company simply mounted it on top, giving the Manning Wardle a very top heavy and decidedly quaint appearance. 'Tertius' nevertheless put in many years of satisfactory service before it was scrapped about 1957.

On many railways, clearances were very restricted, so much so that loco cabs

The Corris and the Talyllyn Railways were close neighbours in Mid Wales and the raison d'etre of both was the carriage of slate, although they were also common carriers. The Corris was closed in 1948 after a bridge was washed away, but the two surviving locos and some of the wagons were preserved on the Talyllyn. This is no. 4 at the buffer stops at Towyn.

21

An Introduction to Modelling Narrow Gauge Railways

The original passenger and mineral railway was of course the Festiniog. One of the line's unique double fairlie locos crosses the level crossing at Penrhyn after preservation.

The promoters of the Vale of Rheidol anticipated a considerable traffic in minerals, but by the early 1920s, all the mines and quarries along its route had all closed. Consequently, for most of its existence, the line has carried only passengers. 'Llywelyn' with a train at Devil's Bridge.

the turn of the century, upgraded itself to a passenger carrier. When extracting the coal became uneconomic, the railway could not survive, services ceasing in 1932.

In England, the Ravenglass and Eskdale in Cumbria is now a 15 inch gauge miniature railway, but it started in the 1870s as a 3 foot gauge line to transport iron ore and lead to the coast. Unfortunately, the mines failed and the company was wound up in 1913.

The last public narrow gauge railway to be built in this country (at least, before steam railways became tourist attractions in themselves) was the Ashover in Derbyshire, which opened in 1924 using 2 foot gauge locos and wagons purchased secondhand from the War Department. It was promoted by the Clay Cross Company to carry limestone from quarries in the Amber Valley to their works and to a junction with the London, Midland and Scottish Railway. As such, the Company had no real wish to carry passengers and general goods, but they were forced into doing so by they had to conform, in theory at least, to the standards laid down by the Board of Trade. They included amongst their number both the first public narrow gauge lines to be built and the last.

Five of these railways were in Wales, the most famous (as well as the oldest) being the Talyllyn and Festiniog, both of which have been preserved. Two of the others were also slate carriers, one being the Corris, a close neighbour of the Talyllyn, whilst the other was the North Wales Narrow Gauge Railway. The remaining Welsh line was the Glyn Valley, a rare example in this country of a roadside tramway, but one which handled a substantial tonnage of granite and also slate and other minerals as well. It closed in 1935.

On the Kintyre peninsular in Scotland, the Campbelltown and Macrihanish started life as a purely industrial line hauling coal, but around

The Cavan and Leitrim, like most of the Irish 3 foot gauge railways, was a common carrier. This is no 4T, a Kerr Stuart 2-6-0T built originally for the Tralee and Dingle, taking water at Mohill on a mixed train to Dromod.(P E K Morgan/GDNGRS Collection)

The 3 foot gauge system on the Isle of Man was one of the first common carrier railways to be constructed and modelling it in 4n12 is much easier nowadays as there are kits for most of the locos by Gem and Branchlines. This elegant Beyer Peacock 2-4-0T was constructed from one of the latter's kits.

Coach and wagons kits for the IoMR are also available from Branchlines, but Roxey Mouldings also make some for the Manx Northern Railway as in this photo.

During the late 1890s, Parliament passed what were known as the Light Railway Acts, which were intended to stimulate the growth of rail transport in areas of the country which lacked such connections. The most important of these became law in 1896 and allowed railways to be built without some of the costly safety measures required of main lines by the Board of Trade. A principal stricture was that speeds were not to exceed 25 miles an hour. It also made the obtaining of powers to construct such lines simpler and, more importantly, cheaper. Until then, every railway had to have a separate Act of Parliament before construction could be started, a process which could be, and frequently was, very costly. Additional finance, in the form of grants from both Government and local authorities, was also made available.

As a result, a great many railways, standard and narrow gauge, were built. The Leek and Manifold in Staffordshire has already been mentioned, but there was also the Welshpool and Llanfair and the Government of the day which wanted to improve rural transport links in the area. The passenger service flourished for only a few years, but quickly fell prey to faster and more convenient buses in the 1930s. Limestone, however, kept the line open until 1950.

Common Carrier Railways

The term 'common carrier', when applied to a railway line, means that it is a public railway hauling general freight and passengers. Many such narrow gauge railways were built to connect a town or open up an area of the country which had so far been missed off the railway network. One of the earliest of these was the Southwold Railway in Suffolk, which linked the small coastal resort of that name with the Great Eastern Railway at Halesworth. The Isle of Man Railway and virtually all of the lines in Ireland also fall into this category. All were 3 foot gauge, although the best known and perhaps best loved, at least amongst railway enthusiasts, was the 2 foot gauge Lynton and Barnstaple in North Devon, which skirted the edges of Exmoor.

David Taylor's freelance Marshwood Vale Railway in 7n16.5 is the epitome of the typical narrow gauge common carrier. (D L Taylor)

An Introduction to Modelling Narrow Gauge Railways

Amongst the best known preserved narrow gauge lines is the Festiniog Railway. One of their unique double fairlies enters Tan-y-Bwllch station with a long train.

the Vale of Rheidol in Wales (although it could be argued that the latter was, at least in intention, a mineral and passenger line as the promoters anticipated a considerable traffic in minerals). It is worth mentioning that the Campbelltown and Macrihanish transformed itself into a fully fledged railway as a result of the Light Railway Acts and that the Ashover was built under their provisions.

Of course, such common carrier railways, serving rural and usually underpopulated areas were particularly vulnerable to competition by buses and lorries, most of them going in the 1930s. In fact, it is surprising that so many managed to last into the preservation era.

Preserved And Tourist Railways

Inevitably, the impression given by the above is that narrow gauge railways are in serious decline. This is in many respects a false one as those lines which lasted long enough to be preserved are now doing a very brisk trade, often carrying considerably more passengers each year than they ever did when they were straightforward commercial operations. Over the past few years, a number of new ones have been built, too, as tourist attractions - usually, but not always, employing locos from industrial lines and/or from abroad. These have sometimes been laid on the trackbeds of lifted standard gauge branch lines, such as the Bala Lake, the Brecon Mountains or the South Tynedale. There are also some rather smaller operations run by groups of enthusiasts, such as the late Reverend Teddy Boston's Cadeby Light Railway or the West Lancashire Narrow Gauge Railway. Other examples are of lines constructed in the grounds of stately homes, such as Knebworth, in theme parks, such as Hollycoombe Country Park in Hampshire and in museums like the East Anglian Transport Museum close to Lowestoft. These are almost invariably 2 foot gauge, the one exception being the Whipsnade and Umfoluzi Railway at London Zoo's annexe in Bedfordshire, which utilises some of the 2 foot 6 inch gauge stock from the Sittingbourne and Kemsley.

There are a few layouts about which purport to represent preserved railways, but I have not seen any which depict a line built specifically to carry tourists, either at exhibitions or described in the model press. In one respect, this is a pity as a layout based on such a railway could be quite interesting, at least, scenically. One built on the trackbed of, say, a closed former Great Western branchline could well have GWR style buildings, signals and the like, but with narrow gauge trains running past them.

The main problem with preserved or tourist lines is that their operation is pretty basic. Usually, trains are run in fixed rakes and merely shuttle back and forth. Indeed, in some cases, where the track is laid in a simple continuous circuit as at Whipsnade, for instance, they just go round and round! On the other hand, with such a railway, it is wholly realistic to run all sorts of different locos together. The Brecon Mountain Railway, for example has a number of locos including (amongst others) a tiny Hunslet 0-4-0ST from a slate quarry, an

Most seaside resorts have miniature railways. The locos are often petrol or diesel engined even if they are steam outline, such as this version of Thomas the Tank Engine on the 7 1/4 inch gauge line at Weston Super Mare.

Modelling Railways Illustrated Handbook No.5

Here and below : Chris Krupa's attractive diorama of a 10 1/4 inch gauge miniature railway. The ticket office and loco shed are based on similar buildings used on the Blackpool Pleasure Beach line, whilst the prototype of the small diesel can be found on the Wells Harbour line and its open coach from Ruislip Lido.

0-6-2 imported from what used to be East Germany and a huge Beyer Garratt 2-6-6-2 from South Africa.

Miniature Railways

Finally, there are the miniature railways, a fair number of which still exist, notably the Ravenglass and Eskdale and the Romney, Hythe and Dymchurch. These were the original tourist railways, although quite a few date from the early years of this century. It is only in recent years that 'proper' railways as such have become of interest to the public at large, so miniature railways had to have some additional appeal. They achieved this by constructing the locos and stock as 'models' of standard gauge ones. Thus, most of the Romney, Hythe and Dymchurch's motive power consists of miniature locos roughly one third the size of the LNER A3 Pacifics.

One of the most common gauges used by miniature lines is 15 inch, although there are others, 7 1/4 and 10 1/4 inches also being popular. The Fairbourne Railway in Wales, for instance, although it started off as 15 inch gauge, was re-laid during the 1980s to 12 1/4 inch and uses small scale replicas of narrow gauge locos.

For the modeller, 15 inch gauge is almost exactly 9mm in 7mm scale and using 4n9 track with modified N gauge locos, a miniature line is quite a feasible proposition. Indeed, some models of Ravenglass and Eskdale stock are being produced commercially in this scale. In 4mm scale, Z gauge track has also been used to model 15 inch gauge lines and it can be used in 7mm to reproduce 10 1/4 inch gauge lines too.

The real disadvantage with choosing a miniature railway as a prototype is that which besets almost all layouts based on hauling tourists, that of a lack

of any real operating potential. There were odd exceptions, however, one being the Ravenglass & Eskdale, which for a time was something of a common carrier and also handled a considerable volume of granite along part of its route. This latter grew to such a level as to justify the laying of standard gauge rails outside the 15 inch gauge ones between the quarry at Murthwaite to the junction with the main line at Ravenglass to avoid the cost of transhipment. A standard gauge Kerr Stuart diesel loco was purchased to handle this traffic and shared the trackbed with the miniature trains.

It is perhaps as well to mention in this section those 15 inch gauge lines which were not actually miniatures. The best known of these were at Duffield Bank in Derbyshire and Eaton Hall near Chester, both being constructed by Sir Arthur Heywood. The former was built on his own estate to demonstrate the practicality of minimum gauge railways as a safe and economical means of transportation, although it also seemed to provide a lot of fun for his family and friends. Much of the route, for instance, was laid out (like many table top toy railways) as a continuous circuit and its rolling stock included both a sleeping and a dining car, hardly essential for a line only about a mile or so in length. The solitary result of Heywood's worthy proselytising was the Eaton Hall Railway, on the estate of the Duke of Westminster. The equipment for both lines was designed and built by Heywood, but they were "proper" narrow gauge, not small replicas of standard gauge locos and stock. Nevertheless, some of them did eventually find their way onto both the Ravenglass & Eskdale and the Romney, Hythe and Dymchurch.

Chapter Four
MODELLING NARROW GAUGE RAILWAYS

A view of Towyn Wharf station from the roadbridge taken in 1980.

As mentioned in Chapter 1, the great glory of the narrow gauge railways of the British Isles is their diversity, which paradoxically, can lead to difficulties when modelling them. Obviously, if one particular line really appeals to you, then there is no problem: you simply choose to reproduce a particular section of it and build the appropriate locos and rolling stock.

Reproducing Part Of A Real Railway

Nowadays, this is rather less difficult than it used to be, for there are a considerable number of books giving a great deal of information which will be of use. However well documented your chosen prototype is, though, you will almost certainly have to undertake some research.

Even if the railway you want to model closed many years ago, it will almost certainly be necessary to visit the area which it served to measure and photograph buildings and other details (assuming they still exist) as the illustrations in books rarely give more than one view of a particular structure. With the passage of time, things inevitably will have changed, often dramatically, and finding sufficient details to build a model of a particular, essential structure, can be difficult.

Research into real railways can be a fascinating branch of the hobby and can lead one into all sorts of equally fascinating byways, so much so that it can become an end in itself and you forget about the modelling! It can also be very

The Greenwich Society's 4n9 model, portrayed as the prototype was in 1969, taken from about the same spot. Note the changes that took place in those 11 years. The site has, of course, altered since.

Most albums of narrow gauge railways include a photograph of the distinctive loco shed on the Snailbeach District Railway from this viewpoint. This shot is of David Brewer's 4n9 version.

The loco and carriage shed at Welshpool in the pre preservation era with one of the line's two original locos posed outside. (P E K Morgan/GDNGRS Collection)

Freelance Modelling

Whilst most layouts are freelance in that they are not copies of a part of a real railway, most standard gauge modellers aim at replicating as closely as possible the practice of particular railway companies. The Great Western enthusiast's fictional station will look like other GWR stations of its type with its elements - the layout of the track, the design of the architecture, fixtures and fittings all following that company's practice.

However, in days gone by, freelancing meant much more than this, and the modeller invented his own railway company, along with its own standard practices. The most famous practitioner of this aspect of the hobby was John Ahern whose 4mm scale Madder Valley Railway (now fortunately preserved at Pendon Museum near Didcot in Berkshire) has been a major influence on model railway enthusiasts for several generations. Although standard gauge, it had much more of a narrow gauge flavour to it. Indeed, some of the stock was actually based on narrow gauge prototypes, even though they ran on 00 gauge track. The Madder Valley was, however, only one of many layouts of this kind: Edward Beal's West Midland line was another, representing another completely fictitious company, this time rather more main line in character than the Madder Valley.

Nowadays, this branch of freelance modelling seems to be largely the preserve of the narrow gauge fraternity, although those who favour standard gauge light railways also have a tendency towards it. In view of the distinctiveness of the prototypes, this is not really very surprising.

The advantage of freelance modelling is that you are not confined to reproducing a particular prototype. If you are modelling, say, the Lynton and Barnstaple, it precludes you having a

frustrating, particularly when you are told that the one person in the local village who had worked on the railway and knew everything there was to know about it, had died the previous week! This actually happened to the author when carrying out research into the Kerry Tramway.

Even if you choose to model a railway which still exists, you can still run into problems. The Greenwich & District Narrow Gauge Railway Society's model of Towyn Wharf on the Talyllyn is as near an exact scale replica as is humanly possible. Moreover, the station is still there to be measured and photographed, which members of the Society duly did way back in 1969. Unfortunately, the prototype kept changing: extensions were added to the buildings, static exhibits were resited, a portacabin erected, a standard gauge siding was lifted and so on. Consequently, the members decided to set the layout in one particular year: 1969, when the site was surveyed.

Modelling a real section of a prototype can be quite rewarding and fortunately, much of the stock of most railways can be built from the considerable range of kits that are now available, particularly in 4n9. 7n16.5 and 7n14 are less well represented, but nevertheless, almost everything needed for quite a few companies is provided.

However, it is perhaps not the ideal kind of layout for the inexperienced modeller, or one new to the narrow gauge scene. It is probably easier to make a start with a freelance or semi freelance layout...

A layout set in a dairy farming area would need cattle wagons, such as this example on the W & L. (P E K Morgan/GDNRS Collection)

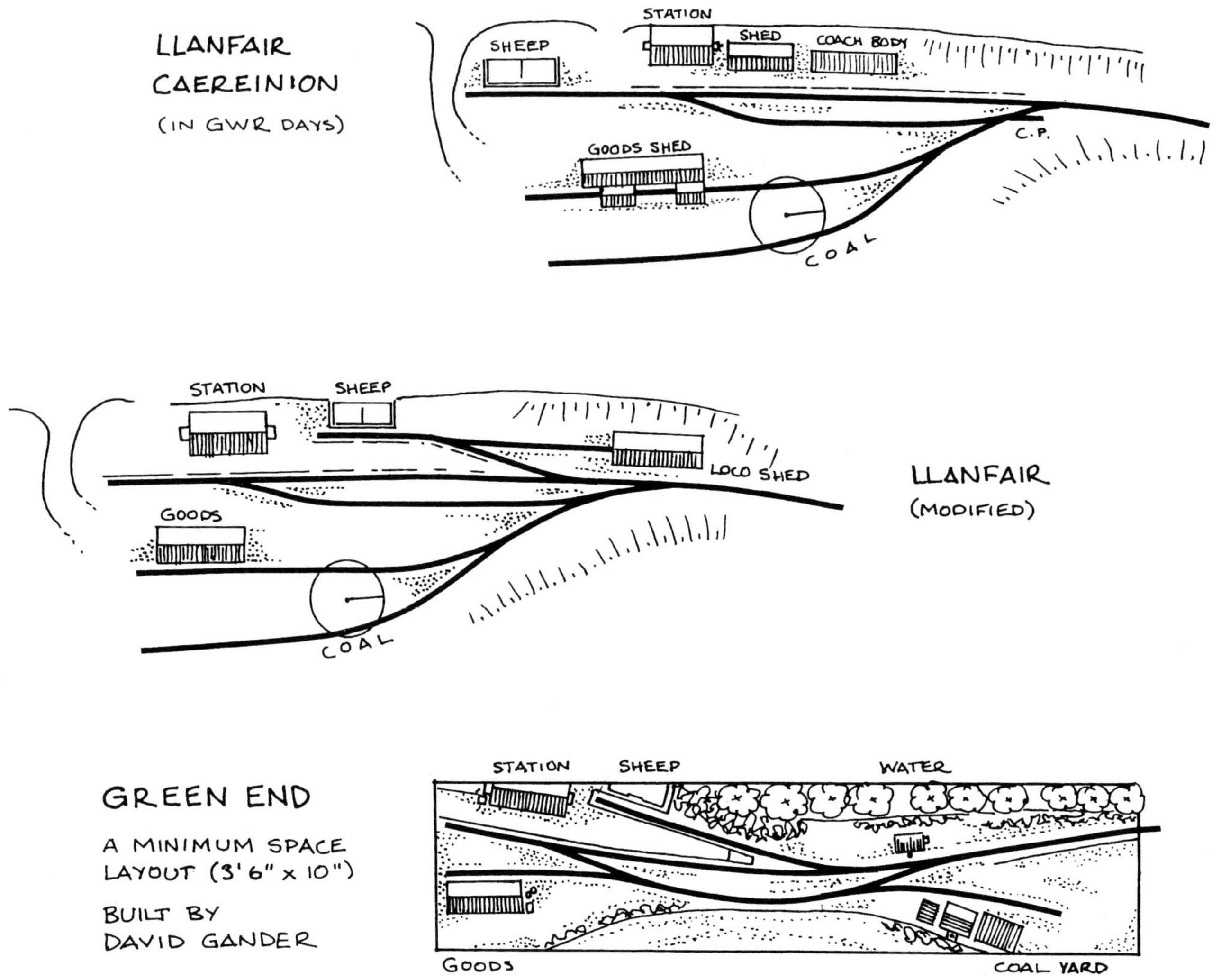

An Introduction to Modelling Narrow Gauge Railways

LLANFAIR CAEREINION (IN GWR DAYS)

LLANFAIR (MODIFIED)

GREEN END

A MINIMUM SPACE LAYOUT (3'6" x 10")

BUILT BY DAVID GANDER

Top : Llanfair Caereinion as it was before the preservation society took over.
Middle : A freelance version of Llanfair Caereinion.
Bottom : Another version of Llanfair which has actually been built by David Gander in 4n9. The dimensions were determined by the size of the bookcase the layout sits on!

Llanfair Caereinion in pre preservation society days with an enthusiasts's special in July 1956 shortly before closure. The line's coaches had long been scrapped, so the passengers were accommodated in the brake vans or on benches in the open wagons! (P E K Morgan/ GDNRS Collection)

Lindal End in 4n9 represents the upper section of the Cleator Railway, a totally fictitious company, but which nevertheless has a detailed route map, a comprehensively researched history and even timetables worked out by its constructor, Barry Jeffery. (George Ansell)

A Hunslet 2-6-2T (from a Parkside Dundas kit) accelerates away from Green End, David Gander's freelance version of Llanfair Caereinion, with a train of Ninelines Plastic kits.(David Gander)

loco which ran on another line, at least if you want to retain prototypical accuracy. Again, few real stations have every facility you might want to model or the train service might be too sparse to offer much in the way of operating interest. In fact, most narrow gauge stations were distinctly lacking both in facilities, the number of trains and the possibilities for shunting.

Take the Welshpool and Llanfair as an example. Before the preservation society took over, it had only two locos and three coaches and was usually run on a 'one engine in steam' basis. Its terminus at Llanfair was pretty basic, consisting simply of a loop and two sidings: four points in all. There was no loco shed, this being situated at the junction with the standard gauge at Welshpool. The track here sprawled quite considerably, so much so that an accurate model of it, even in 4mm scale, would occupy rather more space than most modellers have available. Yet Llanfair Caereinion is quite an attractive prototype, set in the rolling hills of Mid Wales sandwiched between the River Banwy and the road to the village. It would make a good model, but it would be rather more interesting with a few more facilities. A loco shed, possibly a carriage shed or alternatively, a bay to store empty carriages and an extra siding or two would add a great deal, both visually and operationally. Obviously, such a model station would no longer be Llanfair Caereinion.

Paradoxically, the freelance modeller's task in creating a realistic and convincing scene is actually more difficult than that of the one who follows one of the main line companies. Freelancing demands rather more imagination and not a little research as he (or she) has no established practice to guide them.

The easiest way of approaching the planning of a freelance layout is, firstly, to decide what kind of railway you want to model (common carrier, industrial, preserved line etc) and secondly, to work out why such a line might have been built, what traffic it was intended to carry and so forth. Secondly, you have to imagine yourself as the Chairman of the Board of your fictional company and think of how you would go about constructing your railway, equipping and operating it.

The first consideration is really a matter of what appeals to you. Visiting preserved lines, reading railway histories, looking at photographs of prototypes, investigating models and so on will give you some idea of the range. If you have even the slightest interest in narrow gauge, something is bound to attract your attention and inspire you.

The second consideration is to work out some kind of scenario as background to your layout so that you have some form of framework from which to start. Obviously, where your imaginary company is situated will have a major effect on the kind of traffic it will carry. The mountains of Wales inevitably mean slate, at least, to modellers, although this was by no means the only mineral to be extracted in that country, nor was it the only one to be carried on narrow gauge rails.

Very often, personal preference comes into play: a line set in a favourite part of the country might well appeal, in which case, you will need to find out what local industry there was, what

An Introduction to Modelling Narrow Gauge Railways

Had either of the two extensions to the Vale of Rheidol been built, 'Llywelyn' could well have been seen as far afield as Rhayader or Aberayron.

kind of agriculture existed and so on. For example, a line in a part of the country where farming was primarily arable would not need any cattle wagons, whereas one in a dairy farming area would. Obviously, slate wagons would be needed if your railway connected such a quarry with the rest of the country whilst other minerals would be carried in open wagons, hoppers or other specialised vehicles.

Some modellers go to considerable lengths to create background scenarios for their layouts. One of the most comprehensive and believable ones was worked out by Barry Jeffery for his 4n9 Lindal End. Set in West Cumberland (now Cumbria), Barry has plotted the route of his fictional railway from a point near Cleator on the erstwhile London and North Western and Furness Junction Railway to its terminus at Lindal End close to Ennerdale Water. By adapting original timetables, he has devised a connecting service with the standard gauge line and has even printed a pregrouping timetable setting Lindal End under the auspices of the Cleator and Workington Junction Railway. Further details of Lindal End can be found in Chapter 8.

Not all modellers will either want to go into as much detail as Barry Jeffery or wish to take the time to do so. You can simply say, for instance, that your railway runs between Puddlecombe and Much Twittering-In-The-Marsh, two villages situated "somewhere in the West Country" or wherever you choose to set your layout. On the other hand, the kind of detailed background that Lindal End has usually adds something to the model. Your trains may only depart to the hidden sidings, yet these are not simply the inevitable bare baseboards with unballasted track on them, but the other terminus of your imaginary railway. They also move with a purpose, handling the kind of traffic that its prototype, had it been built, would have carried.

Railways Which Might Have Been

Some modellers, rather than invent a purely fictitious line, base their layouts on one of the many proposals for railways which never came to fruition and assume they were actually constructed. This is quite a good idea as it provides a ready made framework to expand on, in that the geography of the area is known and the kind of traffic the line would have carried can be estimated.

There were any number of these 'might have been' railways. The same people who promoted the North Wales Narrow Gauge Railway obtained an Act of Parliament to construct a line between Ruthin and Ceregedrudion and indeed, some earthworks were actually started, but the money ran out before very much progress had been made. Choosing this scheme as a prototype would allow NWNGR type stock, but without tying yourself down to copying the NWNGR exactly.

Another possible imaginary scenario for a model is one of the various proposals to extend the Vale of Rheidol. One involved a lengthy and financially unviable continuation from Devils Bridge to Rhayader. The other was a branch southwards from Aberystwyth parallel to the coast down to Aberayron, a rather more sensible proposition altogether. Needless to add, neither got built.

The Nidd Valley line in Yorkshire was a standard gauge light railway built in connection with the construction of waterworks for Bradford Corporation but at one time it was proposed that it should have been built to 2 foot 6 inch gauge. A similar gauge railway was also planned in Lincolnshire, whilst there were several schemes to lay quite lengthy narrow gauge systems in the West of Scotland. Any of these would make interesting projects for a model, but they are only some of many, the details of which can be culled from the various railway histories.

Facilities for a Freelance Railway

The next stage is to decide on the equipment your line would have. This can be divided into infrastructure (ie buildings) and stock. Is your line to be built on the cheap, possibly as a result of one of the Light Railway Acts? If so, then as Chair-

If your imaginary prototype was built on the cheap, the structures would probably be made out of corrugated iron, such as these at Devils Bridge on the Vale of Rheidol. This view dates from the early 1950s before the freight sidings were lifted and the goods shed demolished. (P E K Morgan/GDNRS Collection)

Modelling Railways Illustrated Handbook No.5

Narrow Gauge in Colour

Above : A run of empty stone wagons begins to ascend the incline on the 7n16.5 Pentre Tramway, having been shunted by a Bagnall 0-4-0ST.
Below : A Meridian Models Ruston diesel shunts wagons onto the Quay on Richard Glover's 4n9 Pagham Harbour.

Above : A Wrightlines Ruston diesel crosses the standard gauge tracks on Maggie and Gordon Gravett's 7mm scale layout, 'Ditchling Green'. An interesting size comparison between the narrow gauge stock and the standard gauge wagon behind. (Gordon Gravett)

Left : A scratchbuilt Fowler diesel with a train of stone wagons passes the loco shed on the 7n16.5 Pentre Tramway. The wagons are also scratchbuilt; the gunpowder van is based on a prototype from a quarry at Penmaenmawr whilst the open tubs are models of those used at Threlkeld in the Lake District.

Modelling Railways Illustrated Handbook No.5

Top : A train of happy holidaymaker's draws into the platform on the Greenwich and District Narrow Gauge Railway Society's 4n9 model of Towyn Wharf.

Above : Narrow gauge railway in a landscape: David Brewer's evocative recreation of the Snailbeach District Railways in 4n9. The loco is 'Dennis', the large 0-6-0T purchased from W G Bagnall & Co, and is seen here collecting an empty coal wagon that has just been lowered down the incline from the power station.

Left : A view familiar to thousands of railway enthusiasts - the roadbridge at the head of Towyn Wharf Station on the Talyllyn Railway. Another scene on the GDNGS' layout.

An Introduction to Modelling Narrow Gauge Railways

Above : A major source of traffic on the author's 7n16.5 Pentre Tramway is pitprops, here being loaded onto some scratchbuilt wagons based on prototypes from the Kerry Tramway. The loco is a Roy C. Link kit.

Below : Kerr Stuart 0-4-2T struggles with a train of empty hopper wagons up the gradient to Snailbeach on David Brewer's 4n9 layout.

Above : The buffer stops at Charmouth on David Taylor's 7n16.5 Marshwood Vale Railway. (D L Taylor)

Below : Along with several other narrow gauge railway companies, the Marshwood Vale Railway purchased an American built Baldwin 4-6-0T from the War Department after the First World War. David Taylor built this 7n16.5 version from a Wrightlines kit.(D L Taylor)

Modelling Railways Illustrated Handbook No.5

Left : A Fowler diesel (from a Nonneminstre kit) on the quayside at Pagham Harbour.

Bottom left : A passenger train draws into Pagham Harbour station. The loco and coaches were constructed from Meridian Models Kits.

Below : A scratchbuilt Hunslet 2-6-2T shunts a private owner wagon in the yard on David Taylor's 7n16.5 layout, Charmouth.   (D L Taylor)

Left: 'Llandydref', Maggie and Gordon Gravett's 7n16.5 layout inspired by the Talyllyn Railway. After entering the tunnel on the right, the train of empty slate wagons will negotiate a tortuous 9 inch radius curve behind the workshops to reach the hidden sidings on the left hand side of the baseboard. (Gordon Gravett)

Below: A passenger train about to disappear into the hidden sidings on David Taylor's 7n16.5 Marshwood Vale Railway. The loco is scratchbuilt and is a model of a 4-4-0T that Hunslets designed, but never built, for the Lynton & Barnstaple Railway. (D L Taylor)

More extensive station buildings at Ballinamore, the headquarters of the Cavan and Leitrim Railway in Ireland. Ex Tralee and Dingle no 3T is involved in shunting a goods train. (P E K Morgan/GDNRS Collection)

Models of the station building and goods shed at Llanfair Caereinion on David Gander's Green End in 4n9.(David Gander)

man of the Board, you would probably opt for structures made out of corrugated iron or timber. On the other hand, if your railway was built to serve a slate quarry, then buildings made out of this material would be readily to hand and just as cheap, if not more so.

Alternatively, you might prefer something a little classier, such as the neat, stone chalets that the Lynton and Barnstaple had erected. You may even be suffering from delusions of grandeur and provide some rather imposing station buildings such as the Isle of Man Railway's headquarters in Douglas or those that some of the Irish companies constructed.

Locos and Stock for a Freelance Railway

One of your many responsibilities as Chairman of the Board will be to determine the kind of stock you will need. This again ties in with where your railway is supposed to be situated. A shortish line without steep gradients and not too much traffic could manage with small, four coupled locos, whereas a longer line through hilly or mountainous country with a lot of heavy traffic would need rather more powerful locomotives.

Most railway companies approached a variety of locomotive and rolling stock manufacturers and asked them to submit tenders for what they required. Naturally, only one of each would be chosen. Thus, the Leeds firm of Manning Wardle provided the motive power for the Lynton and Barnstaple and the Bristol Carriage and Wagon Works the rolling stock. Similarly, Beyer Peacocks won the contract to supply the Welshpool and Llanfair with its locos and Pickerings of Wishaw in Scotland succeeded in gaining the carriage and wagon business. The result of this is that the stock of most companies was fairly uniform and had a certain family resemblance. Too many modellers of freelance narrow gauge railways assume that almost anything goes and mix the stock of a dozen different prototypes regardless of whether they have any similarity of style or even whether they have the same loading gauge or not. In order to be convincing, it is not a good idea to run, say, tiny Talyllyn wagons along with the much larger vehicles of the Lynton and Barnstaple.

There is also a practical problem in mixing the stock of different lines as the height of the couplings above rail level varied quite a lot. This is not so evident in 4mm scale where the difference in height is generally little more than a millimetre or two and can usually be coped with by either packing to lower the coupling or by a bit of judicious carving of the buffer beams. In 7mm scale, however, such devices are rather more noticeable and difficult to fit without major and often unsightly surgery.

This is not to suggest that there should not be any variation at all. Quite a few companies, finding they needed additional equipment, either because they had underestimated what was needed to handle the traffic or because stock had worn out, often chose a different manufacturer to their original supplier.

Due to a strike and the consequent backlog in fulfilling orders, Manning Wardle were unable to provide the L and B with another of their 2-6-2Ts, so the Company was forced to go abroad to the

The stock of most companies was fairly uniform and had a certain family resemblance, as is apparent in this view of wagons on the Vale of Rheidol. (P E K Morgan/GDNRS Collection)

An Introduction to Modelling Narrow Gauge Railways

Both of these 7mm scale models are of the smallest open wagons on two different railways. On the left is a modified Wrightlines Talyllyn style wagon whilst on the right is a Peco Lynton & Barnstaple vehicle. This is dramatic illustration of the variations in the size of the stock of different railways.

A standard design of Hunslets which was supplied in considerable numbers to the Sierra Leone Government Railways. This example is now running on the W and L.

American firm of Baldwin for another locomotive. By the early 1920s, the Corris needed a replacement for one of their original locos, but the builder, Hughes of Loughborough, had long ago ceased trading, so the Management purchased a loco from Kerr Stuart. Happily, this still survives as æEdward Thomas on the Talyllyn.

After the First World War, a huge amount of railway equipment was sold by the War Department, most of it being 2 foot gauge. A substantial number of locomotives had been obtained from the United States, largely because British loco manufacturers could not supply them in the quantities needed quickly enough. Several British lines acquired some Baldwin 4-6-0Ts to supplement their motive power, the Glyn Valley, Welsh Highland and the Snailbeach having four between them, whilst all of the Ashover's stud consisted of these ugly, but utilitarian machines.

Had, for example, the Scottish firm of Andrew Barclay tendered successfully for supplying the locomotives for your layout, then the chances are they may well have produced an 0-6-2T exactly like the two they supplied to the Campbelltown and Macrihanish. (Barclays, in fact, included a picture and description of one in a catalogue they produced, describing it as a class P loco - this assumes they were required to work the same kind of traffic over a similar route to the C and M). In this instance, you can simply build models of the Barclay 0-6-2Ts, but repainted in your own freelance company's livery. (Chivers Finelines used to produce a kit in 4n9).

On the other hand, you can use models of one of the many standard designs that most loco manufacturers produced for export. A great many of these were for narrow gauge railways abroad, India being one of the main markets, but there were (and still are) examples of British built machines at work all over the world. Choosing such motive power would probably involve 'anglicising' the design, ie, removing double roofs on cabs, cowcatchers and other equipment not normally fitted on British railways. There are some suitable kits of such locos available: Parkside Dundas produce one in 4n9 for a 2-6-2T which Hunslet supplied in considerable numbers to the 2 foot 6 inch Sierra Leone Government Railways, whilst Roxey Mouldings sell several Hawthorn Leslie designs for the Cyprus Government Railways, also 2 foot 6 inch gauge.

Other railways, primarily those constructed before the Light Railway Acts and which had quite a lengthy lifespan, such as the Festiniog and the North Wales Narrow Gauge Railways, had a fair old variety of coaches and wagons. The former had its tiny 4 wheeled quarrymens' coaches running with some rather swish and comfortable bogie vehicles, all to several different designs. The NWNGR also had a very diverse lot of coaches, ranging from 4 wheelers via some very rough and ready looking 6 wheelers to some relatively modern bogies. Again, these were built by several different manufacturers, each having their own distinctive styles.

Working out this kind of background for a freelance railway may seem like a lot of hard work and it does demand a fair amount of research because, even though you are building a model of a totally fictitious railway, it still has to be railway-like both in appearance and operation. On the other hand, freelance

Another British loco produced for export, but which is suitable for a freelance railway is this model of one of the handsome 2-6-2Ts manufactured by Hawthorn Leslie for the Cyprus Government Railway. A Roxey Mouldings whitemetal kit in 4n9, it is designed to fit a Farish N gauge chassis.

One of the best examples of semi freelance modelling: Maggie and Gordon Gravett's Llandydref in 7n16.5. (Gordon Gravett)

The 7n16.5 Pentre Tramway is based, albeit loosely, on the Kerry Tramway. These model buildings are copies of those served by the prototype.

modelling of this kind does exercise your imagination and if done properly, can be very satisfying.

Semi Freelance Modelling

If you do find inventing the kind of fiction necessary for a totally freelance layout rather daunting, or if you are specially attracted to one prototype in particular, but don't want to tie yourself down totally, then there is the alternative of what I term 'semi freelance' modelling. This simply involves taking a prototype railway and freelancing it to suit your own circumstances or preferences. The advantage is that the prototype provides you with a realistic and ready made framework in which to work.

Examples of this kind of modelling can be found in Chapter 8, one of the best being Maggie and Gordon Gravett's Llandydref in 7n16.5. The Drefor and Pentre Tramways also fall into this category.

Llandydref is a station on an imaginary common carrier-cum-slate railway in Wales and draws heavily on the Talyllyn for inspiration. Indeed, most of the passenger and freight stock and some of the motive power is TR in origin. The setting itself is, however, completely fictional. Llandydref bears little resemblance to Towyn, yet the layout convinces, partly because of the standard of modelling, but also because the Gravetts have put some thought into the overall theme of the layout and have stuck to it. Although not all the locos are models of TR prototypes, they are all more or less the same size and have a common loading gauge.

The Drefor and Pentre Tramways (in 4n9 and 7n16.5 respectively) might also be described as semi freelance, but to a lesser extent than Llandydref. Both were inspired by the short-lived Kerry Tramway in Mid Wales and although the layout of the track in both cases is freelance, almost all the structures are models of buildings served by the Kerry. The scenery, too, is reminiscent of Mid Wales.

Album Layouts

Some narrow gauge modellers don't want either to model a section of a real railway or to build a freelance line, so they tend to go in for what have been called 'album' layouts. These act simply as scenic backgrounds on which stock from a variety of different prototypes appear, usually in their correct liveries. A Festiniog train, for example, will appear alongside a Glyn Valley one, which will be followed by a Lynton and Barnstaple loco and coaches and so on. Hence, the term 'album' layouts: the procession of trains across the layout are an album of different prototypes.

Although such layouts are not representative of one particular railway, either freelance or real, this does not imply that the modelling need necessarily be of a low standard or uninteresting. Quite the opposite is true: one of the best layouts of this kind is David Gander's 'Nantgwyn' in 4n9 which is very well detailed and as a result, deservedly popular on the exhibition circuit.

Album layouts are not for everyone, but they are useful if you don't want to paint your locos and stock in freelance liveries, construct a copy of a real line or tie yourself down to only one prototype. Their one disadvantage is that operation tends to be rather limited as most operators of such layouts tend to keep models of one particular company's stock separate from those of another. Consequently, opportunities for shunting are rather restricted.

David Gander's Nantgwyn is an excellent example of an Album layout. Here a World War One train of WD stock is hauled by a German 'Brigadelok' (a Duton kit imported by Meridian Models). (David Gander)

Chapter Five
TRACK

Stub points at Coed-y-Parc on the Penrhyn Slate Quarry railway. (P E K Morgan/GDNGRS Collection)

As in most matters to do with narrow gauge railways, the kind of track used by different companies varied quite considerably.

Only a few railways went in for chaired track, that is with the rails (bullhead in profile) sat in cast chairs bolted to wooden sleepers, notably the Festiniog, Penrhyn, Dinorwic and Croesor lines. Most railways, however, used spiked track, usually with flat bottomed rail sitting directly onto the sleepers and held in place by dog spikes, although others employed clips and bolts to keep the rails in gauge. Sometimes, a flat metal plate, known as a soleplate, was inserted between the rail and the sleeper to spread the weight of the locos and stock more evenly. The Talyllyn used a curious combination consisting of part spiked rail, but with every fourth sleeper fitted with chairs.

On industrial lines, several different systems were used. Some older railways used bridge rail, which in profile looked like an inverted U, whilst others used what was known as bar rail. This consisted simply of metal bars inserted into a slot cut into the sleepers.

Some railway equipment suppliers offered (and still do) ready made, portable track. This is very much like the rigid set track that comes in model train sets. The rails are attached to preformed steel sleepers and come in short lengths, either straight or curved and are assembled in pretty much the same fashion as model railway track laid on the carpet! Hudsons of Leeds are the main producers of such track, although there were plenty of others, John Fowler and Co. and the French firm, Decauville.

A peculiarity of some industrial railways was the stub point. Unlike a conventional point, it has no closure rails and sometimes, no check rails or crossing vees. The rails are simply moved across and the crossing vee (or frog) is usually, but not always, replaced by a pivoted length of rail. The accompanying photographs should make this clear.

Modelling Considerations
Using track intended to represent standard gauge in a scale smaller than the one you are modelling in, is frankly unrealistic as the sleepers will be too small and too narrowly spaced. The only possible exceptions are if you hide the sleepers under grass or ballast or use it only in hidden sidings or tunnels or any other location which is out of view. In any event, there is no real need to use such track as there are at least two very acceptable ranges of flexible narrow gauge track and points available.

The market leader is undoubtedly that produced by Peco in both 4n9 and 7n16.5, both of which give a reasonable depiction of spiked track. The sleepering is moulded to represent badly worn and rotted timbers and as such, is ideal to depict a line with trackwork in a terminal state of decay. With careful painting and ballasting, the results can be very realistic. The only criticism of it that might be made is that the rail in the 4n9 range is code 80 (the same as that used in Peco's N gauge track) which is rather overscale and a bit heavier

Stub points in model form on Pete Wilson's 'Chwarel Cwm Bach' slate quarry in 4n8.(Roy C Link)

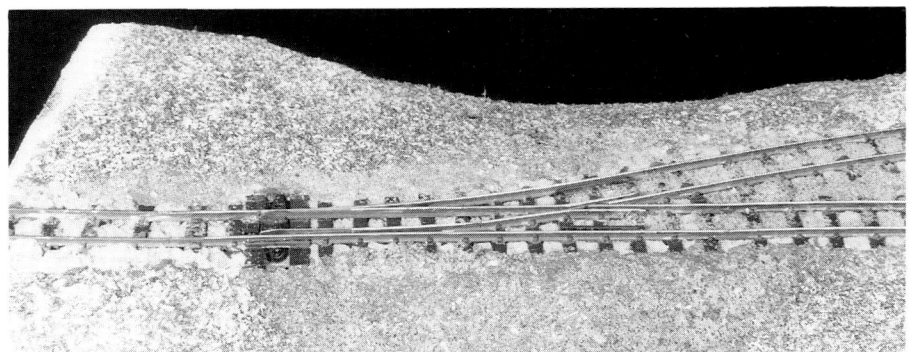

Although there is still a lot of work to be done scenically, this view of a 4n9 Peco narrow gauge point shows how the overscale rail is not too noticeable after ballasting. This is a view of an industrial layout under construction. The ballast is supposed to be 4mm scale mud - actually Carr's furry plaster mix.

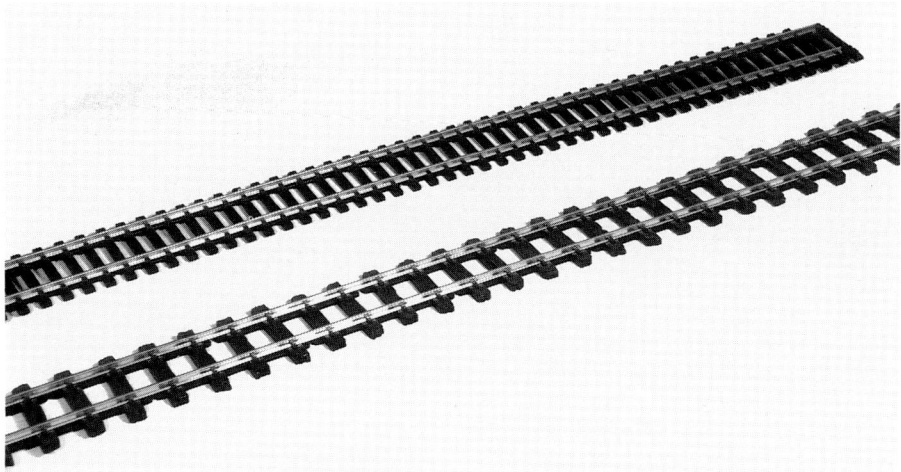

Peco 7n16.5 track alongside standard 00 gauge track from the same manufacturer. The rail size is the same, but the difference in the sleepers is obvious.

than is necessary for almost all N gauge wheels. In the days when I modelled in 4n9, I used Peco Z gauge rail when scratchbuilding track and had no problems with even the coarsest wheels. In 7n16.5, the rail used is code 100 which is almost spot on for the heavier section rail used by some narrow gauge common carrier railways.

The German firm of Bemo also produce narrow gauge track in both 3.5n9 and 3.5n12 which can be readily used for 4n9 and 4n12 respectively. This represents track maintained to a rather better standard than that depicted by Peco in that the sleepers, whilst moulded with a wood grain effect, look rather less 'bashed about'. If you are modelling a narrow gauge railway which is either newly constructed or prosperous enough to maintain its track properly, its worth having a look at this range. If you want 12mm gauge ready made track, its also the only one available. As it is manufactured in Germany, it is a bit more expensive than Peco and is not quite so easily obtainable.

The Austrian firm of Roco also make 9mm gauge track in both normal and industrial styles.

Occasionally, it is possible to purchase other ready made track, usually 9mm gauge and usually produced in Japan, but it is worth checking that it is truly 9mm gauge. Some years ago, along with some other members of the Greenwich & District Narrow Gauge Society, I bought some very nice looking track made in the Far East for a 4n9 layout we were constructing. Its principal attraction was the small section rail used. After it was laid, we discovered, to our horror, that the stock kept falling off and on checking the gauge, found it was actually 0.5mm wider than it should have been.

For those interested in industrial railways in 7n14, Roy C. Link produces a range of components to build Hudson type portable track. Although you have to assemble the track yourself and supply your own rail, it is no more difficult with these components than, say, building a whitemetal loco kit. The instructions, along with templates, as usual from this manufacturer, are very comprehensive and easy to understand. The components themselves consist of plastic sleepers moulded to represent the pre-formed steel sleepers of the prototype with holes in them. Small dog spikes are inserted into the holes to hold the rail in place. Apart from plain track, there are also packs of sleepers available to build points.

Again in 7mm scale, Branchlines produce some etched brass rail fittings based on examples used on the Lynton and Barnstaple, but which can be adapted for any gauge of track.

Finally, it is worth mentioning that scratchbuilding track and pointwork is not that difficult. The easiest method is to solder rails to copper clad sleepers, the resulting track being very strong indeed. Pre cut sleepers can be purchased from a variety of sources and there are also point templates available as an aid. Making your own track by this method is much cheaper than buying it, which is the only reason why I do it.

Accurate 14mm gauge Hudson portable track in 7mm scale constructed from Roy C Link's components on Adit 2. (Roy C Link)

An Introduction to Modelling Narrow Gauge Railways

Chapter Six
COUPLINGS

The sideframes of Talyllyn wagons were extended to form dumb buffers. Coupling was effected by hooks and chains. (P E K Morgan/GDNGRS Collection)

By now, it will come as no surprise at all to learn that there were almost as many methods of coupling stock together as there were narrow gauge railways.

The Talyllyn was one of the few lines to follow standard gauge practice, with locos and passenger stock fitted with sprung side buffers and central screw couplings. Wagons had dumb buffers formed by extending the side frames beyond the ends of the wagon bodies. This was quite a common arrangement on industrial systems too, actual coupling being effected simply by means of hooks and chains. Instead of conventional sprung buffers, locos were usually fitted with two large wooden blocks of wood faced with metal plates on each buffer beam, with a coupling hook and chains between them.

The disadvantage of a pair of buffers, either dumb or sprung, on lines with very sharp curves and rough trackwork, was the need for the couplings to be very slack, otherwise the wagons could be easily derailed. Unless couplings are taut, there is a great deal of banging and crashing of the rolling stock in normal operation and consequently, an increased likelihood of damage. Many narrow gauge railways consequently went in for some kind of combined buffer and coupling arrangement located in the centre of the buffer beam. The most sophisticated version of this, usually found on the more recently constructed common carrier railways, was the 'Norwegian chopper', which was used by such lines as the Lynton and Barnstaple, the Welshpool and Llanfair, the Vale of Rheidol etc. Sometimes, the Board of Trade insisted that these couplings be supplemented by safety chains on either side of the chopper.

In modelling, chopper couplings have one other significant advantage in that their use generally avoids any tendency for the stock to 'buffer lock', when buffers move out of alignment and their faces fail to coincide, leading to derailments and damage to stock. On locomotives and long wheelbase stock, the choppers usually need to be pivoted, (as they do on the prototype), although it is not always necessary on short wheelbase wagons.

This is by no means a comprehensive survey of the many different buffer/coupling systems used on the real thing, but the photographs show some of the variations.

A number of industrial lines utilised the same system. These are 7n16.5 models of the inside framed wagons used on the 2 foot 4 1/2 inch gauge railway at Threlkeld Quarry in the Lake District

The 18 inch gauge stock of the Woolwich Arsenal was fitted with a more sophisticated double buffer system.

Most narrow gauge railways used a single buffer centrally located in the buffer beam as on this Festiniog wagon. (P E K Morgan/GDNGRS Collection)

Couplings in 4mm Scale

From very early on, manufacturers in both 3.5n9 and 4n9 settled on a standard coupling for narrow gauge stock and this is still the one most commonly used by modellers. It consists of a central buffer with a projection at the centre and a metal loop which engages with the projection on the adjacent coupling. Most of the very wide range of kits in this scale either have versions of it or make allowance for such types to be fitted.

The standard coupling is designed to couple automatically and also uncouple by means of uncoupling ramps. However, in the days when I modelled in 4n9, I could never persuade them to couple automatically. The other problem was that the metal loops were invariably too short, although this could be solved by a little judicious bending with a pair of miniature pliers. The other disadvantage of the standard coupling is that it is quite large and when fitted to the smaller stock of lines like the Talyllyn, the Festiniog and Corris, for example, it looks very overscale. Nevertheless, with a bit of adjustment, it works well and is readily available. Peco produce a version, but Bemo and Liliput versions can be obtained through Parkside Dundas, amongst others.

Some time ago, Meridian Models introduced a whitemetal version of the chopper coupling, complete with an etched brass coupling hook. These are a vast improvement in appearance over the standard coupling, but suffer from being very fiddly to use both because of their small size and that of the stock. Coupling and uncoupling is manual, using a small screwdriver or hook.

Other modellers, particularly those who prefer 'hands off' operation, employ one of several automatic coupling systems intended for N gauge. These are larger than the Meridian Models choppers, but rather less obtrusive than the standard coupling. All allow for auto-

A typical Norwegian chopper coupling on one of the Sittingbourne & Kemsley's locos, although the massive housing projecting from the buffer beam is not.

An Introduction to Modelling Narrow Gauge Railways

The standard 4n9 coupling as produced by Bemo fitted to a Ninelines Welshpool and Llanfair wagon. (David Gander)

matic coupling and all uncouple by means of magnets laid between the rails. Three are of etched brass: the MBM, the B and B and the DG coupling. The latter two also incorporate an optional device to permit delayed uncoupling, whereby vehicles can uncouple over a magnet and then be pushed without recoupling. All three are compatible with the standard 009 coupling.

The other couplings some modellers use also have a delayed uncoupling feature. These are produced by the American firm, Kadee, but can be obtained in this country from model shops which specialise in importing model railway equipment from abroad, notably Victors of London and M.G. Sharp of Sheffield. The Kadee is a miniature of the knuckle jawed couplings fitted to American prototypes (and these days, to some British standard gauge multiple units). They

Above: Automatic B and B couplings in use on 4n9 wagons. The one on the right over the uncoupling magnet buried under the track as evinced by the raised loop, whilst that on the left is in the normal position ready for coupling. (Richard Glover)

Left: Meridian Models scale chopper coupling in 4n9 looks much more prototypical than its competitors.

46

are made largely of plastic (although obviously with some metal components), are neat and unobtrusive and work moderately well, though they are rather more expensive than the home grown etched variety.

None of these couplings are a 100% reliable, but the more care taken when fitting them and the better they are maintained, the more efficient is their operation. Their use does, however, distort the operation of layouts to a greater or lesser extent. The movement of trains and the shunting of stock is largely dictated by the positions of the uncoupling magnets, whereas real railways suffer no such constraints. This can be minimised by careful and plentiful distribution of magnets about the layout. For those who don't like the 'Great Hand In The Sky' descending from the heavens to couple and uncouple models, automatic couplings are of course infinitely preferable.

Couplings in 7mm Scale

In 7mm scale, it is possible to use couplings which are more like the real thing, although their operation can still be fiddly. Wrightlines produce whitemetal castings of the chopper coupling in several different styles: a Lynton and Barnstaple type, a War Department type and a freelance one with a large square buffer. No hook is provided and some means of making and fitting them has to be devised. However, it is possible to adapt the WD style coupling by fitting a loop and soldering a spigot behind the buffer head for the loop of the neighbouring vehicle to engage with. The result is very much like the standard 009 coupling in action, but very much neater and more prototypical in appearance and is also very reliable.

An etched brass version (with hook) is available through the 7mm Narrow Gauge Association. This is a kit and is freelance in design, but still looks very convincing.

These apart, there is no standard 7mm scale coupling as there is in 4mm. Modellers use a whole range of different types: quite a few use Kadees, whilst others employ any one of several couplings intended for 4mm standard gauge models. Some even use the standard 009 coupling, for in this scale its appearance is acceptable. My 7n16.5 Pentre Tramway stock has largish industrial type buffers with a spigot glued in. Coupling is effected by means of small, loose brass loops, either dropped on or picked up by a pair of very fine tweezers. The system works well (with practice) and is also prototypical (see accompanying photograph).

Kadee N gauge coupling fitted to a 7n14 Roy C Link skip chassis.(Roy C Link)

The system used on the author's 7n16.5 Pentre Tramway...

Right : ... and a similar method in use on prototype industrial wagons.

Chapter Seven
NARROW GAUGE LOCOMOTIVE KITS

Etched brass kits are often avoided by beginners as they usually need to be assembled using a soldering iron. However, this Branchlines railcar in 7mm scale is very simple to construct and is ideal for a first attempt

Hardly an issue of almost any of the model railway magazines goes by without at least one article on assembling a kit. Indeed, there are even a couple of books on the subject by no less a person than the editor of Modelling Railways Illustrated, Iain Rice. If you have never tackled a kit before, then this welter of words can make the business seem very complicated and something to be avoided at all costs.

Undoubtedly, the most daunting kits for the newcomer are locomotives, yet there is no need to be put off. It is as well to remember that a kit is no more than a few bits and pieces which need to be stuck together. Many of them, especially those in 4n9, consist of less than a dozen parts in all. Those with more are not necessarily more difficult - often there is only a bit more sticking to do.

By far the most common material used in narrow gauge loco kits these days is whitemetal, though there are an increasing number of etched brass ones about. Some have parts made from both materials whilst others at the top end of the market also include lost wax brass castings, which tend to be much finer and more accurate than those in whitemetal. Those kits which employ different materials generally make more realistic models, but are inevitably rather more expensive. Whitemetal and brass castings are ideal for bulky parts, such as boiler fittings, cylinders and the like, whereas etched brass is better for representing sheet metal, like weatherboards, cabsides and so on.

Nevertheless, kits utilising parts from only one material can still be made into excellent models as most manufacturers use a number of dodges quite successfully to overcome the apparent shortcomings of the particular material they use. One favourite is for whitemetal cabsides to be bevelled at the edges to give the illusion that they are much thin-

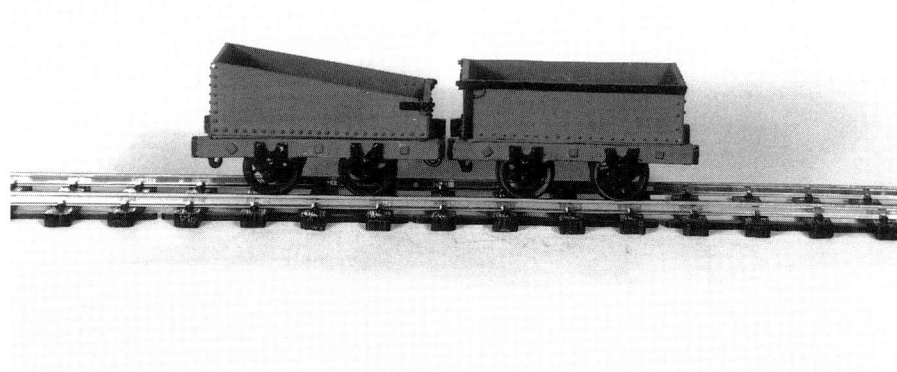

Before tackling a loco kit, it might be as well to tackle one of the simpler wagon kits in whitemetal such as these Wrightlines Talyllyn ones in 7n16.5. Each consists of a mere 8 parts (plus wheels).

One of the smaller Chivers Finelines kits would probably be a good choice for a first attempt at constructing a 4n9 whitemetal loco. This example is running on Christopher Krupa's layout, Minbury Abbas.

ner than they actually are. Some of the parts, too, are exceptionally finely detailed and elevate casting almost into an art form.

What has not yet appeared in narrow gauge kits in the UK, although it has in some of those aimed at the standard gauge market, is cast resin. This is widely used in the military modelling world and is capable of producing accurate and very highly detailed parts. It is lighter than whitemetal (which in certain circumstances gives it a significant advantage), but is not quite as strong. It is mentioned because some enterprising kit manufacturer will doubtless produce a kit with some parts made of it in the not too distant future. Indeed, one French narrow gauge firm (Duton) has imported some models made from it already.

Plastic is most widely used in wagon and coach kits. In 4n9, its use is the rule rather than the exception - a pity because some of the smaller wagons (such as industrial tippers) would benefit from underframes of a heavier material, a feature which would radically improve their track holding capabilities. It has not been used in the manufacture of loco kits, and because of the costs involved, probably never will.

One of the simple whitemetal kits designed to fit onto a commercial, ready to run chassis is probably the ideal kit for the beginner to tackle first. Before doing so, it would be a good idea at first to have a go at a whitemetal coach or wagon, or a road vehicle or lineside feature of some kind. These are often very easy, have only a few parts and will teach you a lot whilst you are making it. Even if you make a hash of it, it won't be the end of the world as most are relatively cheap.

The first loco I ever completed (many years ago now) was a 4n9 kit by Rodney Stenning, for one of the attractive Lynton and Barnstaple 2-6-2Ts. This was stuck together, if I remember correctly, with Evostick impact adhesive and I don't recall having any problems at all. The 009 Society in their Handbook suggest that Peco's Glyn Valley Tramway loco would be suitable for a first attempt, although when I asked around other members of the Greenwich and District Narrow Gauge Railway Society, the general consensus of opinion was that one of the smaller Chivers Finelines kits would be an even better proposition.

In 7n16.5, the S & D Dick Kerr petrol electric loco (designed for a Hornby chassis) employs what the manufacturer describes as a 'screw 'n glue' method of assembly. Each part has small tabs with holes in them which interlock with similar tabs on its neighbours. Small screws can be inserted into the holes of these tabs, so holding the parts together whilst gluing or soldering. Other kits

Like the prototypes, model loco kits can be modified. This is another Chivers Finelines saddle tank which has had its cab altered to a pillar type and had a lot more detail added.(David Gander)

I've assembled in this scale which I think a beginner could cope with are the Wrightlines Ruston diesel (to go on a Tenshodo or Hanazono SPUD unit) and the same company's Barclay A class 0-4-0T, intended for a Dapol pug chassis, although the latter is a little more difficult. The Springside 'River Collection' is designed very much with the beginner in mind. It consists of four different loco kits, all of which have some parts, such as the boiler and the footplate, in common, and all of which are designed to fit readily onto the Dapol pug chassis with hardly any modification. The resulting models are described by Springside as 'characterisations', i.e., they are freelance, but they appear to be based, even if only loosely, on locos produced by W.G. Bagnall.

Glue versus Solder

The experts tend to advise soldering whitemetal kits together rather than gluing. It can sometimes be easier (if you are experienced at it) and does tend to result in a stronger model, a factor

Peco Glyn Valley Tramway loco in 4n9 designed to fit a readily available Graham Farish chassis.

An Introduction to Modelling Narrow Gauge Railways

The S & D whitemetal kit for the War Department Dick Kerr petrol electric loco in 7n16.5 utilises a "screw and glue" method of assembly. It is intended to fit on a Hornby chassis, although this example sits on a scratchbuilt one.

Several locos which operated in the Pen-Yr-Rhosedd slate quarry were fitted with toolboxes almost identical to the one on this Wrightlines whitemetal kit in 7n16.5. On this model, it masks the motor of the Dapol pug chassis on which it is designed to sit. The prototype, a Barclay A class, was, however, never used at Pen-Yr-Rhosedd.

A 7mm scale Wrightlines kit of a Motor Rail Simplex industrial loco in whitemetal sits on a Tenshodo Spud which needs virtually no modification.

which is quite important given that a fair number of models end up being accidentally dropped at some stage in their lives! However, for the beginner, using an adhesive of some kind is, in my view, a good deal more preferable.

An ordinary soldering iron will melt whitemetal, if operations are not exceptionally quick, and you will therefore need to invest in one with temperature control, and these can cost more than the kit itself. Soldering, too, seems to be one of those skills which a great many people shy away from, even though it is less difficult than, say programming a video, at least in my experience!

For the record, what I do these days is solder the main body components together and use epoxy resin for everything else. As it takes a few minutes for the epoxy to set, it allows sufficient time to ensure that chimneys, domes and other fittings are vertical and in line and adjust their positions if necessary.

A fast setting two part epoxy resin, such as Araldite or Humbrol (I prefer the latter as it does not seem to string so much) is usually recommended. The major advantages of epoxy are its strength and its gap filling properties. Whitemetal parts rarely fit absolutely perfectly and some filling of joints is usually necessary, but if you use epoxy and are lucky, it will do the job for you. Any excess which squeezes out of the joint can be removed with a modelling knife, but this is best done before the epoxy fully cures, some five to ten minutes or so after the joint has been made. None of the makes of the '5 minute' resins, by the way, do actually set in such a short time. There is one further advantage to epoxy resin in that it can be dissolved by a proprietary paint stripper such as Nitromors. If you do make a mistake, you can simply dunk the offending parts overnight and they should have separated by the following morning.

Incidentally, many constructors of kits who write in the model press suggest using car body filler on whitemetal models, something which strikes me as madness as this stuff is very hard and requires a lot of sanding to get a perfect finish. This is, firstly, hard work and secondly, risky in that the chances are that you will damage other areas of the model in the process, rivet detail being especially vulnerable in this respect. I use Milliput, not the standard grade, but the variety described as 'superfine'. This is not as hard and is therefore easier to sand if necessary, but its principal virtue is that it is water soluble, at least until it has set. Consequently, it can be used to fill awkward joints where sanding is virtually impossible, such as between boilers and cabs fronts and around boiler fittings. Once stuffed into place, the excess can be wiped off with a damp cloth and sanding can be wholly avoided.

As mentioned in the Introduction, this Handbook is not a 'how to' book and I don't intend adding to those thousands of words already written on assembling kits. With so many different models in different scales and gauges and employing different methods of construction, it would in any case be impossible to cover the subject comprehensively. It is, however, worth reading as much as you can, even articles dealing with models of prototypes you are never ever likely to want. I always make a point of doing so and have picked up all sorts of tips and wrinkles which have proved useful. You may never want a model of a Ruritanian State Railways broad gauge single wheeler, but you might find the method of fitting a left handed widget to the inner sprocket of one useful when you are scratching your head trying to work out how to fit one to your prize Hunslet or Manning Wardle. The aforementioned books by Iain Rice are also worth investing in even though he deals wholly with standard gauge kits, as they do provide a comprehensive account of all the major techniques used in whitemetal and etched brass kit construction.

Using Ready To Run Chassis

There remains an aspect of narrow gauge loco kit construction, which poses difficulties rarely associated with standard gauge locos. Most of the latter these days seem to come with their own chassis but the majority of narrow gauge kits do not, being designed to fit onto commercial ready to run chassis intended for a scale or two smaller. Thus, 4n9 kits are powered by the chassis of

One of the large Hunslet 0-4-0STs with outside frames at Dinorwic Slate Quarry. (P E K Morgan/GDNGRS Collection)

Whitemetal kits for 'Cackler' are produced in 4n9 from Chivers Finelines and in 7n16.5 by Peco. Branchlines produce an etched chassis kit with outside frames to go under the latter as an alternative to the inside framed Hornby chassis it was originally designed for

Kits for the Talyllyn Railways 'Dolgoch' are available in 4n9 from Gem and 7n16.5 from Wrightlines.

N gauge models and 7n16.5 ones by 00 gauge locos.

For the beginner, this is obviously advantageous as it saves time and, more importantly, doesn't frighten off those who have never built a chassis before. Indeed, my suspicion is that not that many narrow gauge modellers actually construct their own mechanisms at all. Frankly, if I can find a suitable RTR chassis to go under whatever I am constructing, whether it's a kit or a scratchbuilt project, I will do so. Chassis construction is not as easy as it is sometimes made out to be and like soldering, is something that a lot of people won't tackle. There have been times when I wished I was one of them, but that may well be because I am more than a little cack-handed!

That said, using a chassis intended for a loco in a smaller scale under a narrow gauge body inevitably involves some sort of compromise with prototypical accuracy. The diameter of the wheels and their spacing, for instance, may well be wrong, even if only by a couple of millimetres or so, but in 4mm, this is a scale 6 inches and the resulting model can end up looking rather badly proportioned. In 7mm scale, where 2mm is just over 3 inches, this will be correspondingly less and may well not be readily noticeable.

What will be noticeable, though, will be the number of spokes, for standard gauge locos are usually rather better endowed in this respect than their smaller counterparts. In 4mm scale, this is not all that obvious, partly because of the small size of the models and partly because the motion and valve gear tend to obscure the wheels, but it is a different matter in 7mm. This is also a problem faced by scratchbuilders as there are hardly any wheels available commercially which are suitable for narrow gauge locos.

Other compromises may also have been made by the manufacturer in order to accommodate the motor or some other part of a particular RTR chassis. Either the basic dimensions of the loco body have been altered or alternatively, a toolbox or some means of masking an awkward protrusion will have been provided. Quite a few real locos were fitted with additional toolboxes, sandboxes or whatever, so this latter device is, in my view, preferable to tampering with the proportions of the model as a whole.

To my mind, however, the biggest problem with using RTR chassis is that all the ones currently used for kits are inside framed, whereas a considerable number of narrow gauge prototypes had frames located outside the wheels. This was to enable fireboxes (and the ashpans fitted beneath them) to be accommodated between the frames.

Track gauge was the deciding factor. For example, most of the smaller Hunslet 0-4-0 saddle tanks had fireboxes 2 foot 8 inches wide which sat between the frames and those designed for use on 2 foot gauge obviously had outside frames. There were some, however, which were used on 3 foot gauge railways and these had inside frames. This was not a hard and fast rule as practise varied from loco builder to loco builder, some having fireboxes which sat on top of inside frames rather than between them. The 18 inch gauge locos built for the LNWR's Crewe Works and those for the LYR system at Horwich

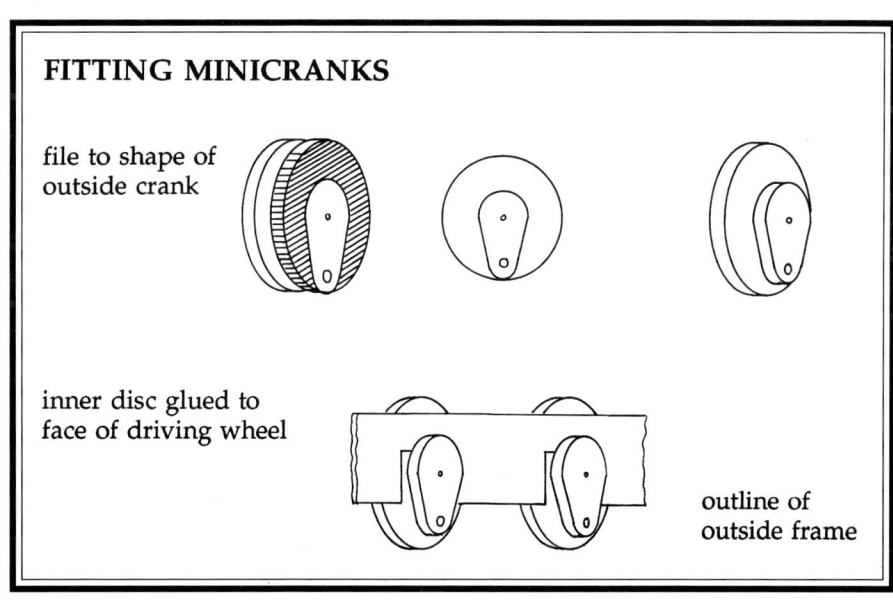

FITTING MINICRANKS

file to shape of outside crank

inner disc glued to face of driving wheel

outline of outside frame

An Introduction to Modelling Narrow Gauge Railways

fell into this category. Bagnall of Stafford frequently made use of a circular marine type firebox which could be readily mounted on top of the frames, so a fair number of their products were inside framed.

Nevertheless, a great many of the locos running on railways of about 2 foot 6 inch gauge and under (and in some cases, over) had outside frames, particularly the larger 6 coupled variety which were most frequently found on common carrier lines. The Lynton and Barnstaple, the Vale of Rheidol, Leek and Manifold, Welshpool and Llanfair all had exclusively outside framed locos, whereas other companies only had some examples of this type. Almost all the kits

Backwoods Miniatures produce a range of high quality loco kits in 4mm scale, one of them being this Vale of Rheidol 2-6-2T which comes with its own outside framed chassis.

All brass Roy C Link kit for a Lister petrol loco in 7n14. A milled brass chassis is included. (Roy C Link)

of outside framed prototypes which sit on RTR chassis look rather top heavy and more than a little odd, at least to my eyes. If you are dependent on RTR chassis, then one solution is to choose kits of prototypes which were also inside framed, but this will inevitably restrict what you run on your layout. On the other hand, you may well feel that an incorrectly framed model of your favourite loco is better than no model at all.

There are a couple of ploys to overcome the outside frame problem, at least in 4mm scale, but I would not advise the newcomer to try them on their first kit. One is to replace the axles which come with the RTR chassis with extended ones. Gears, wheels and motion have to be removed and then refitted on the new axles, which also need new cranks and false outside frames as well.

The other is to use what are known as 'minicranks', which used to be available (and apparently still are from time to time) from Saltford Models. The accompanying drawings illustrate what they are. One of the circular faces is filed to the shape of an outside crank, whilst the other is glued with epoxy resin to the face of the driving wheel on the RTR chassis. Again, motion and valve gear have to be removed and replaced on the new outside cranks.

Although I haven't tried either of these methods myself, I do know modellers who have used them successfully and seen the results operating reliably, both in their own homes and at exhibitions, which is the real test. Given the heavy modifications to the chassis required, it might be better to wait until you have some experience before attempting to tackle such projects. The vast improvement in appearance is certainly worth the effort.

It may be possible to use these methods in 7mm scale, although I must admit I've never seen or even heard of anyone trying them. Minicranks probably wouldn't work anyway. The only reason they do in 4n9 is that the majority of N gauge chassis are gear coupled, with the coupling rods being purely cosmetic. Consequently, no great stresses are placed upon them. Most 00 chassis, however, are not gear coupled and rely on the connecting rods to make the driving wheels go round, so the stresses on those epoxied-on cranks will obviously be greater. However, an increasing number of kits in 7mm scale do come with their own chassis or, if not, another manufacturer sells a suitable alternative. Branchlines, for instance, produces an outside framed etched brass chassis kit to go under the Peco whitemetal body of a large Hunslet, one of several available from this producer.

Availability

There is one final problem which does arise with the use of RTR chassis and that is availability. Manufacturers are legally bound to state on their labels what additional parts (including chassis) are needed to complete their kits, so you can easily find out which one a kit is designed for. However, kit makers (who are usually only one or two man operations) have no connection with the much bigger companies who produce 00/H0 and N gauge models whose chassis are utilised. These big companies usually have their own production schedules which take no heed of either the kit manufacturers or we narrow gauge modellers. Consequently, models are sometimes made in relatively short production runs and supplies of them can suddenly dry up or alternatively, a particular model can simply be deleted from their range. Even worse is when one of these companies goes bust.

A few years ago, a Spanish firm, Ibertren, began importing a range of N gauge models at very low prices, including a small 0-4-0T which prompted several narrow gauge kit manufacturers to design models to suit it, Unfortunately, Ibertren recently ceased trading to the detriment of both modellers and kit producers alike. The moral of this story will be obvious.

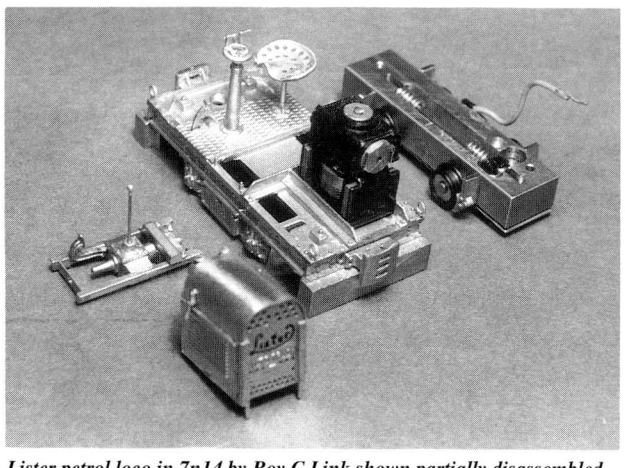

Lister petrol loco in 7n14 by Roy C Link shown partially disassembled.

Modelling Railways Illustrated Handbook No.5

Chapter Eight
EXAMPLES OF NARROW GAUGE LAYOUTS

A Bagnall 0-4-0ST (scratchbuilt on an Arnold N gauge chassis) positions flat wagons by the timber drying sheds on the 4n9 Drefor Tramway.

Reading about other peoples' layouts and/or seeing them at exhibitions is usually of great interest to other modellers, even if you don't like or think much of what they have done or how they have gone about things. On the other hand, in my experience, some of the best layouts can inspire you to try to achieve a higher standard, although they can also drive you to despair when you contrast them with your own efforts!

The layouts described (albeit briefly) in the following pages have been selected to illustrate a range of approaches to narrow gauge modelling. Some are freelance, some represent a prototype, some are semi freelance whilst others don't fall easily into either of these categories. What all bar one have in common is that indefinable, but essential ingredient, atmosphere: the exception is my own Pentre Tramway, which I will leave others to judge!

The Drefor Tramway (4n9)
The Drefor Tramway was built by the author and two other members of the Greenwich Society (Richard Clover and Christopher Krupa) and is based loosely on the erstwhile Kerry Tramway, one of the more obscure of the Welsh narrow gauge railways. This was a 2 foot gauge line built on an estate at Kerry, near Newtown, in 1888. It carried timber, slab stone and agricultural produce for some seven years before it was lifted, only to be re-laid again in 1917 to extract timber for the war effort.

There was not enough information on the line to build an accurate copy of any part of it, even if the three members

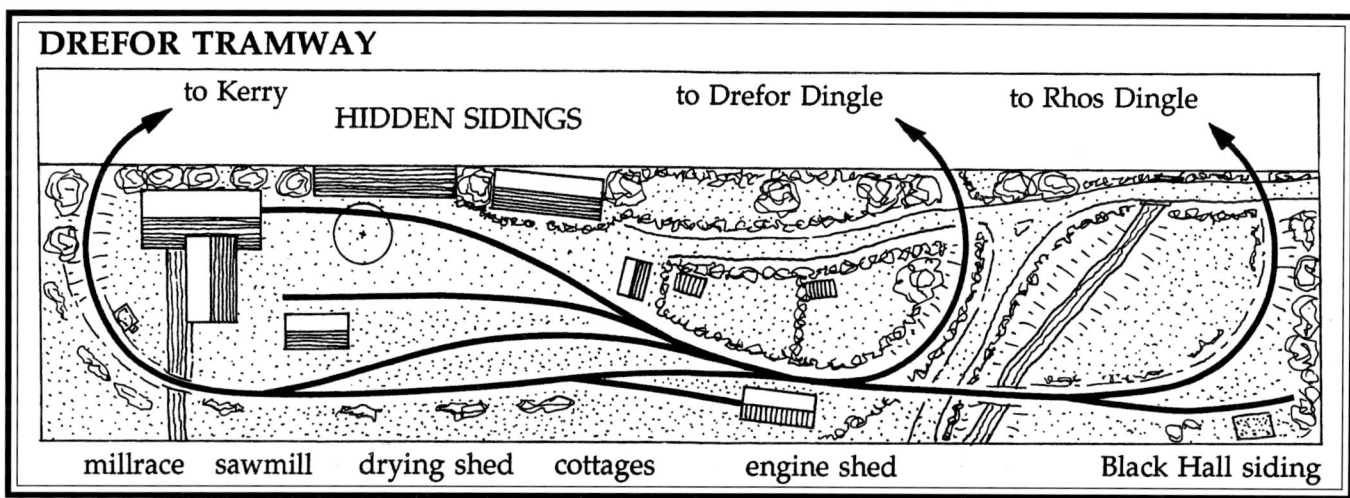

53

An Introduction to Modelling Narrow Gauge Railways

A modified Gem Barclay E class waits outside the smithy.

involved with the layout had wanted, so they invented the freelance Drefor Tramway, Drefor being the name of a farm alongside the real tramway.

The layout occupies three baseboards, each three by two and a half feet and the trackplan was designed to show some of the major features of the route of the real Kerry Tramway. As can be seen from the accompanying plan, the track basically consists of a continuous circuit, with another representing one of the several branches that existed on the prototype. However, the layout is never operated as a continuous run, nor is it apparent that the track forms a circuit of this kind when viewed from the front, as the hidden sidings are masked by a backscene.

Operations centre on the sawmill complex, which is a model of part of one once served by the Kerry. Logs are brought down from the various plantations (represented by the hidden sidings) to the sawmill and sawn timber is then loaded and delivered down the line to the junction with the standard gauge, which is also presumed to be offstage in the hidden sidings. Like the real Kerry Tramway, the Drefor also serves a quarry as well as handling agricultural traffic for the various farms on the estate on which it is situated. At one end of the layout is a siding especially for this.

The motive power consists of several small 4 and 6 coupled locos, some kitbuilt with one or two scratchbuilt items, all constructed on commercial RTR chassis. Although none of the prototypes ran on the real Kerry Tramway, they are all suitable for such a line, being the standard designs that various firms constructed for industrial use. The rolling stock consists mostly of ex-War Department wagons built from plastic kits by Parkside Dundas. Again, such vehicles did not run on the prototype

A Barclay E class wanders through the Mid Wales countryside en route to one of the logging areas. The loco was modified from a Gem kit of 'Douglas' on the Talyllyn

A stone train approaches the sawmill yard on its way to the junction with the standard gauge behind a scratchbuilt Bagnall saddle tank on the 4n9 Drefor Tramway.

A scratchbuilt Bagnall 0-6-0T brings a train of stone off the Drefor branch

Many timber railways used these Bagnall 0-4-0STs and the Pentre Tramway is no exception.

tramway, although they were used on other timber carrying lines.

The Pentre Tramway (7n16.5)
Having completed the Drefor Tramway, the author moved up to 7mm scale and rather than change prototypes, simply constructed another version of the Kerry. This layout is also freelance and hence has been christened the Pentre Tramway: Pentre, like Drefor, is an area around Kerry through which the 'real' Tramway passed.

The design for the 7n16.5 version represents a different approach to that of Drefor, being intended for a different space. Longer and narrower, it is some 15 foot by 22 inches at its widest point.

Although the Pentre Tramway is freelance, its history is very similar to that of the Kerry. It, too, started life sometime in the 1880s and was constructed to serve a country estate. Unlike the Kerry, however, the quarry it ran to developed into a larger scale enterprise and the line survived continuously up to the late 1920s/early 1930s. The period depicted on the model is immediately after the First World War (i.e. the early 1920s) when a number of temporary branches had been laid to woodlands to extract timber.

Again, operations are based largely around the sawmill, but subsequent research into the prototype revealed that much of the timber cut in the area was used for pitwood, which was sawn to length by small, portable mills close to the site of felling. Consequently, only some of the timber hauled out of the various plantations (represented by the hidden sidings) is delivered to the sawmill. Nevertheless, wagons loaded with pitwood do appear on the layout, as it is assumed that a branch to one or more plantations diverges in a trailing direction from the route to the junction, with the standard gauge just offstage in the hidden sidings. Locos have to run round their trains by the sawmill before departing again. Other timber is loaded at the opposite end of the layout, where there are a couple of sidings to handle the agricultural and general traffic on the estate.

The Kerry Tramway had several inclines, but although there was no room to include any on the Drefor Tramway, it proved possible to squeeze one in on the Pentre. Only part is modelled, the top end disappearing behind trees and bushes, so enabling wagons to be loaded out of sight. It is assumed that the stone quarry is situated at the top of the incline. Apart from empty wagons being sent up to the quarry and full ones descending the incline, gunpowder for blasting and coal to power the quarry machinery are also hauled up periodically.

Along with Christopher Krupa, I've spent a considerable amount of time researching the Kerry Tramway and as more information about it has come to light, it has proved necessary to rebuild the model. The sawmill complex, for instance, has had to be rebuilt and virtu-

An Introduction to Modelling Narrow Gauge Railways

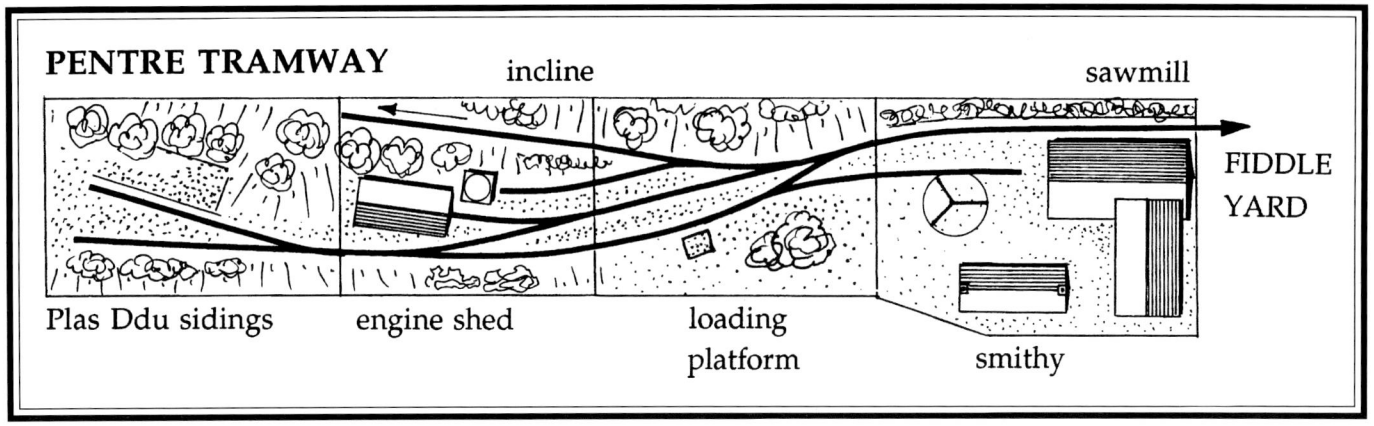

A scratchbuilt 0-4-2IST, based on the prototype built by Bagnalls for the Kerry Tramway, waits as empty wagons are hauled up the incline.

The prototype of this Fowler 'Resilient' class was manufactured a decade or so after the real Kerry Tramway was lifted, but nevertheless, this scratchbuilt model is a useful member of the Pentre Tramway's motive power stud.

Modelling Railways Illustrated Handbook No.5

Bagnall 0-4-2IST emerges from between the trees with an empty stone train. After running round, the loco will shunt the wagons to the incline to be hauled up to the quarry for loading.

View of the rebuilt sawmill complex.

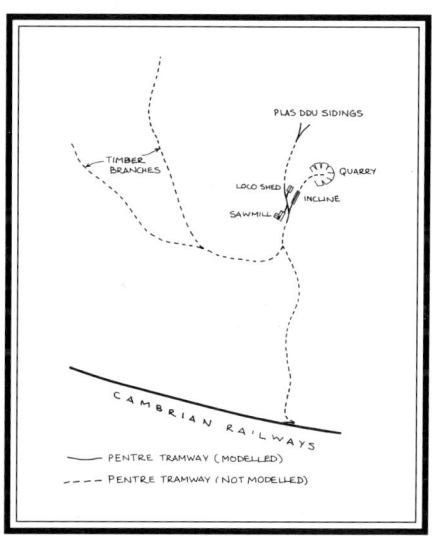

A wagon loaded with logs descends the incline.

An Introduction to Modelling Narrow Gauge Railways

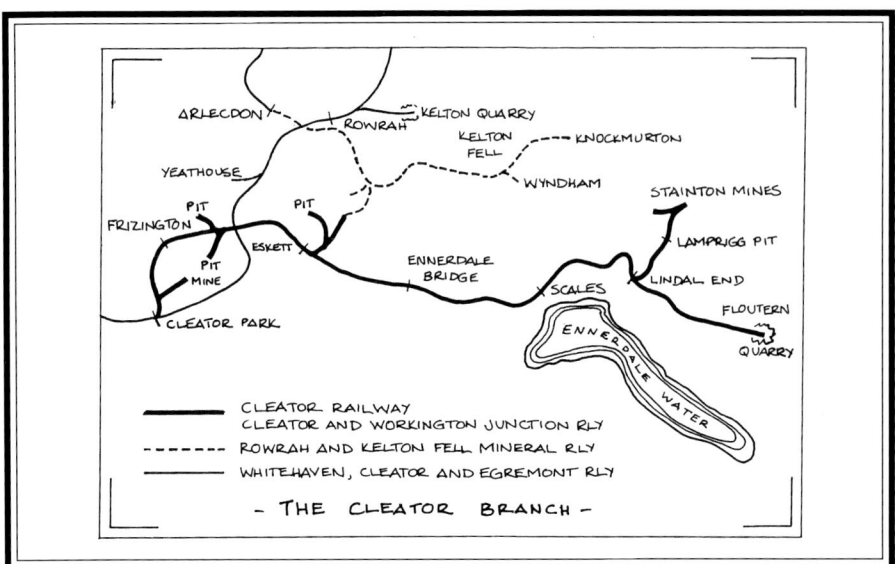

ally all of the rolling stock is in the process of being replaced. This has all had to be scratchbuilt, so it has taken (and will take) quite a few years to complete.

Lindal End (4n9)

Lindal End represents part of the upper section of the Cleator Railway, a 2 foot 3 inch gauge line in Cumberland. It was opened in 1876 running from the standard gauge at Frizington station (renamed Cleator Park Junction) via the village of Frizington itself, Eskett, Ennerdale Bridge and Scales to Lindal End itself. It was constructed to tap the haematite iron ore deposits at Frizington Moor and Ennerdale, but also carried slate from quarries above Lindal End. (North Wales is not the only area where slate was quarried). In 1882, the railway was taken over by the Cleator

Behind the goods vehicles can be seen the shed where the Stainton Mineral Branch loco is shedded overnight. (George Ansell)

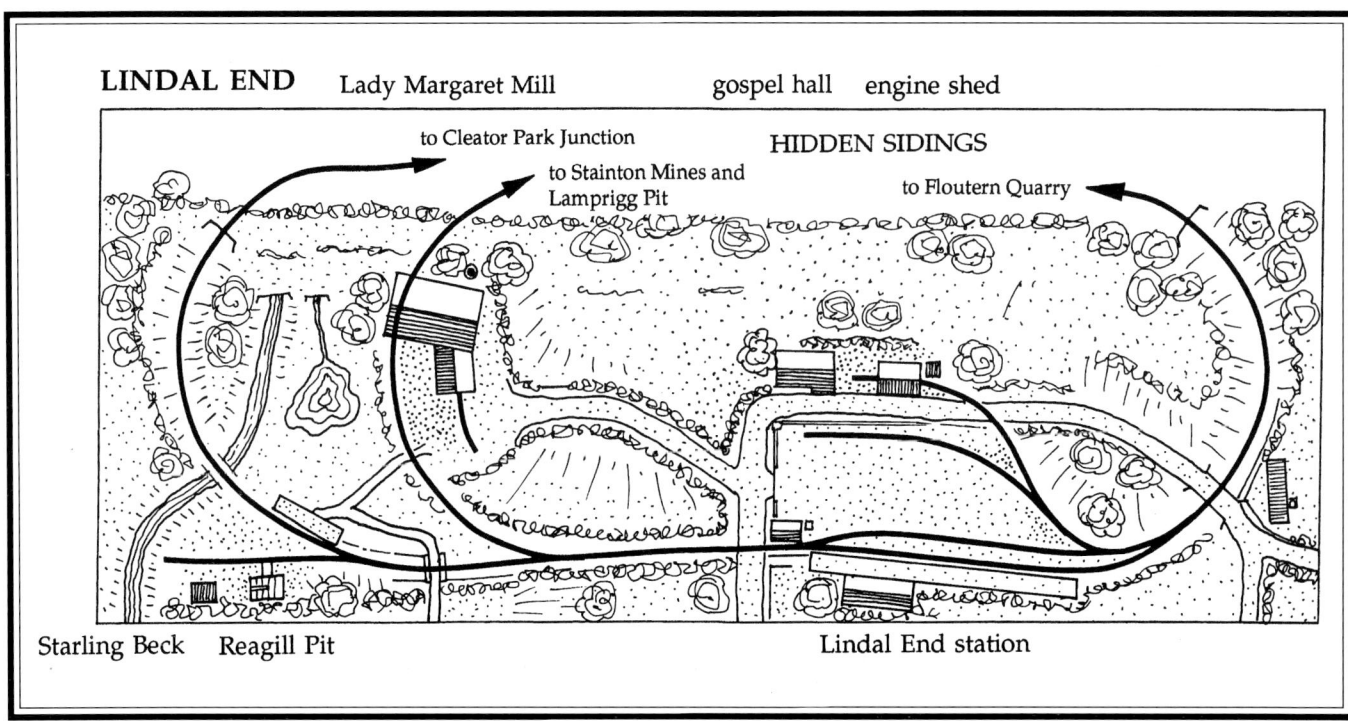

Modelling Railways Illustrated Handbook No.5

An overall view of Lindal End with the goods yard in the middle and the Stainton Mineral Branch curving away from the main line to Cleator Park Junction in the distance. (George Ansell)

and Workington Junction Railway which was in turn absorbed by the London, Midland and Scottish Railway, at the time of the grouping.

Almost all of the above is pure fiction, being the product of Barry Jeffery's imagination, yet the Cleator Railway could quite easily have existed. Its course was plotted on an old Ordnance Survey map and its history written after studying the local railway situation. The Cleator and Workington Junction Railway, for example, did actually exist and was incorporated into the LMS in 1923.

Having established the background to the layout, it was a relatively easy task to decide on the stock requirements. Mineral wagons for the haematite and slate wagons were an obvious necessity, but general and agricultural freight was also carried. There are four trains a day on the Cleator Railway, timed to connect with the standard gauge trains at the junction, although there is an extra trip on Wednesdays and Saturdays for Ennerdale market. On summer Saturdays, there is an additional service to meet the through coaches of the LNWR's holiday express.

A glance at the accompanying track plan will show that Lindal End is virtually a mirror image of that of the Drefor Tramway. Barry adopted that of the Welsh model for his layout because it offered him the most scope operationally.

Yet Lindal End is very different to Drefor, both scenically and, perhaps surprisingly, operationally as well. Trains from Cleator Park emerge from the tunnel leading to the hidden sidings at the rear and pass a halt with a short siding to a haematite trial pit known as Reagill Pit Halt. There are other mines served by the railway and just beyond Reagill Pit is the Stainton Mineral Branch serving Lamprigg and Stainton Pits, both offstage. Mineral trains enter here from the hidden sidings. Lindal End station is the limit of passenger services, but the railway continues for a short distance to a slate quarry at Floutern Tarn. The scenery is very evocative of the area

A view of Reagill Trial Pit from the rear of the layout with ex War Department wagons (from Parkside Dundas kits) for carrying haematite. The period modelled is the 1930s, by which time the Cleator Railway had been absorbed by the LMSR. (George Ansell)

An Introduction to Modelling Narrow Gauge Railways

A goods train from Cleator Park Junction passes Reagill Pit Halt en route to Lindal End. The loco is from a Chivers Kit. (George Ansell)

elling Review' for designing layouts which would fit on a sheet of A3. David Barham won second prize, but when he actually got down to building the model, adopted the slightly larger A2 size to give himself a little more space: hence Adit 2...

Despite its small size, Adit 2 does have a fair amount of operational interest. Locos bring trains of empty V skips from the hidden sidings at the rear of the layout, run round them and then propel them one by one to the entrance to the adit. This is too steep for locos to use, so the wagons have to be let down the incline by means of a chain. A small stop scotch holds each skip in place while the chain is attached. Once the skip is out of sight 'below ground', it is loaded through a small hole at the back of the baseboard with a removable load of waste stone. It is then hauled back up the incline by the chain where it is collected by the loco. Once a complete train of skips has been dealt with in this fashion, it is taken back to the hidden sidings where the loads are taken out and the whole cycle is ready to be repeated. Variety is introduced by running trains carrying supplies: cement, portable track, oil drums and the like.

The stock, like the track, is built from Roy C Link kits and consists mainly of V skips. These are made of plastic and are consequently very light, so small lumps of lead have been added, hidden beneath false floors. Flat and bolster wagons, based on the same skip chas-

of Cumberland which borders the Lake District. The extraction of haematite is not the most environmentally friendly of activities, the areas around the pits being covered in a red dust which gets everywhere. This has been well captured on Lindal End, but without overdoing or exaggerating the effect. Trackwork is Peco and the layout is a compact 8 foot by 2 foot.

ADIT 2

An adit is a short tunnel which leads to a mine or tunnelling project of some kind. Adit 2 is therefore one of several adits dug in connection with the construction of a water main between a reservoir and an electricity generating plant. Many schemes like this involve the digging of a number of adits, to increase the number of working faces and so hasten the tunnelling process. After completion,

A train, on its way to Lindal End, winds round the curve off the Stainton Mineral Branch past the derelict Lady Margaret Pit which masks the exit to the hidden sidings. (George Ansell)

they are either sealed or used for maintenance, or as valve shafts.

Adit 2 is not necessarily the second adit along the tunnel, but it actually refers to the size of paper! The plan was submitted for a competition run by 'Narrow Gauge And Industrial Railway Mod-

sis, handle all the other traffic. Locomotives are all small industrial diesel and petrol types as befits a temporary contractor's line of this nature. The mainstays are a Ruston LAT and a Lister (both Roy C Link kits), a Motor Rail Simplex and a Fowler Marshall

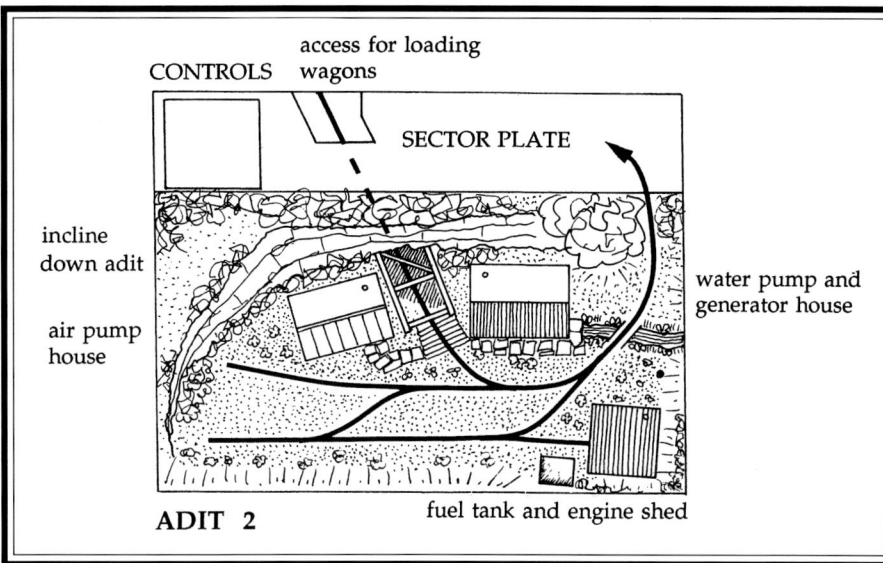

erated by the quarry company's own motive power and stock. Passenger services alternate with stone trains from an imaginary quarry half way up the line in the hidden sidings. Mineral trains emerge from there and enter the loop, where the loco uncouples and moves off to an isolating section. The stone is transferred from the wagons to ships at Pagham, but offstage, along the kickback road from the loop. This crosses the creek (the tide always seems to be out at Pagham!) by means of a rickety wooden trestle which heavy locomotives are forbidden to cross, so loaded and empty wagons have to be hauled or propelled between the station and the unloading point by a lighter internal combustion loco, usually either a heavily modified armoured Simplex or a Ruston from Wrightlines and a scratchbuilt McEwan Pratt, the prototype of which dates from about 1919.

Couplings are the smallest available Kadees which are intended for N gauge, but which work well with the very small locos and stock on Adit 2.

Pagham Harbour (4n9)

There was actually a station at Pagham in West Sussex, though it was served by a standard gauge light railway, not by a narrow gauge one. Other than the name, it shares nothing with Richard Glover's minimum space layout in 4n9, which is purely freelance.

The model Pagham Harbour is the terminus of a small narrow gauge railway situated 'somewhere on the Sussex coast'. It is a common carrier with some mineral traffic, although the latter is op-

Right : Adit 2 : A Ruston LAT diesel grinds slowly round a curve with a single flat wagon in tow between the loco shed (which has full interior detail) and the water pump and generator shed on the left.(Roy C Link)

Below : Adit 2 : A loaded skip emerges from the adit. Note the high level of detail in this scene: the planking around the track, the pipes (through which air and water were pumped) into the adit, the bicycle and the general debris around the site.(Roy C

(both of which are made from Meridian Models kits). These manoeuvres, along with the running of conventional passenger, general goods and mixed trains, ensure that Pagham is quite an entertaining little layout to operate, even though it has a mere four points.

Stock is all built from kits and again, the locos are all of the small, 4 coupled variety which suits the size of the layout as a whole. Automatic B and B couplings are used. Track is scratchbuilt from Peco code 80 rail soldered to PCB sleepers.

Charmouth (7n16.5)

Charmouth is a real village in Dorset, but the Marshwood Vale Railway which connects it to the former Great Western station at Bridport (which closed in

An Introduction to Modelling Narrow Gauge Railways

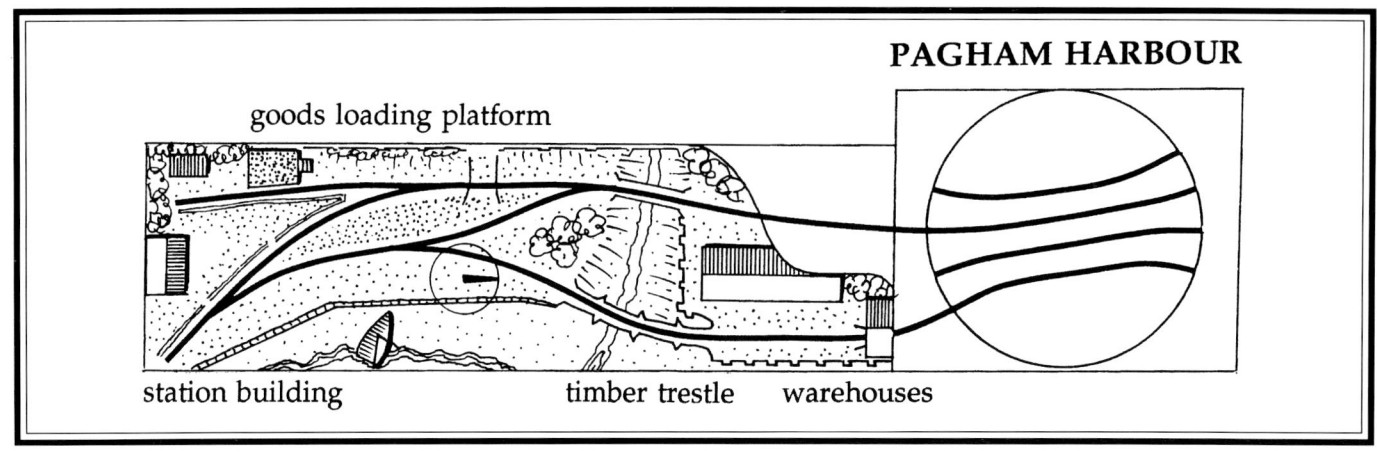

A Meridian Models Ruston diesel waits on the quayside at Pagham Harbour for a mineral train to arrive.

A mineral train emerges from the hidden sidings into Pagham Harbour station.

Modelling Railways Illustrated Handbook No.5

The entrance to the hidden sidings at Pagham is masked by this large warehouse.

1975) is the invention of David Taylor. Envisaged as a common carrier line, the MVR provides the scenario for his small, entirely freelance layout representing the line's terminus at Charmouth. As with Lindal End, the railway's route has been plotted on an Ordnance Survey map running through the villages of Symondsbury, Broadoak, Shave Cross and Whitchurch Canonicorum.

Like most convincing freelance models, all the stock, passenger and freight, has been constructed to a common style and loading gauge, so that there is some continuity of appearance and style, just as real railways have. Everything has been scratchbuilt, including much of the motive power. Only one of David's locos is from a kit and that is the Wrightlines Baldwin 4-6-0 which the MVR, in common with several prototype lines (Glyn Valley, Welsh Highland and the Ashover) purchased after the First World War from the War Department. The rest of the MVR's loco stud consists of a Hunslet type 2-6-2T and two locomotives for which the designs exist but which were never actually built.

Hunslet submitted a tender to supply the locos for the Lynton and Barnstaple Railway back in 1897, but were unsuccessful, so the engines they designed for it were never constructed. David used one of the surviving drawings of a rather elegant 4-4-0T to scratchbuild a model for the MVR. The

The passenger train waits as the mineral train draws into the loop at Pagham Harbour.

An Introduction to Modelling Narrow Gauge Railways

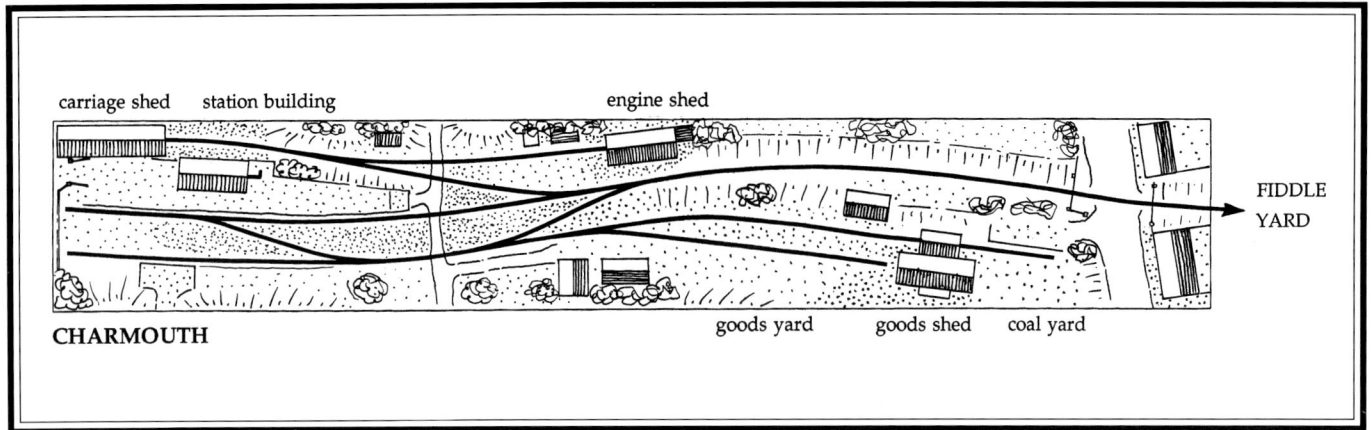

A scratchbuilt Hunslet 2-6-2T on shed at Charmouth (D.L.Taylor)

other loco on the railway's roster is a single Fairlie designed by James Spooner (of Festiniog fame) for another railway in North Wales which never got built.

Charmouth is 13 foot 6 inches long by 1 foot 8 inches wide, not large by any means. Plain track is Peco with handbuilt points with the rails spiked to wooden sleepers and the locos and stock are fitted with Airfix or Fleischmann couplings.

Snailbeach (4n9)

The name, Snailbeach District Railways, is evocative of the kind of whimsical line that the late Roland Emmett might have invented. In fact, Snailbeach is a real place and the SDR continued to exist until very recently, even though the track had been lifted long ago. Latterly, its sole source of income was from wayleaves paid by Shropshire County Council whose lorries used the trackbed to transport crushed stone from a quarry.

A view of the goods yard at Charmouth with scratchbuilt wagons. On the right is the goods shed, whilst in the middle of the picture is the goods office. The structures, made of timber and corrugated iron, are typical of those on cheaply constructed lines. (D L Taylor)

Modelling Railways Illustrated Handbook No.5

Charmouth : David Taylor's beautiful scratchbuilt model of the single fairlie that was designed by James Spooner (of Festiniog fame) but which was never built. (D L Taylor)

David Brewer has long been interested in this obscure, but fascinating little mineral railway and his layout is an increasingly accurate portrayal of part of it. When it was originally planned, a couple of minor additions were made to the track plan to make operation more varied. In its later days, the prototype operated a mere three trains a week. Stone from the quarry was carried in wagons which moved by gravity down to the standard gauge at Pontesbury, but every other day saw one of the three locos steamed up to collect the empties and take them back up the line to the loading point. Obviously, to do this in model form would be tedious in the extreme, so a loop was added by the loco shed and a timber branch included to some imaginary plantations. Although fictitious, this was not entirely unreasonable as during and just after the First World War, a great deal of timber was felled in the area and one or two horse powered narrow gauge railways were laid to extract the logs.

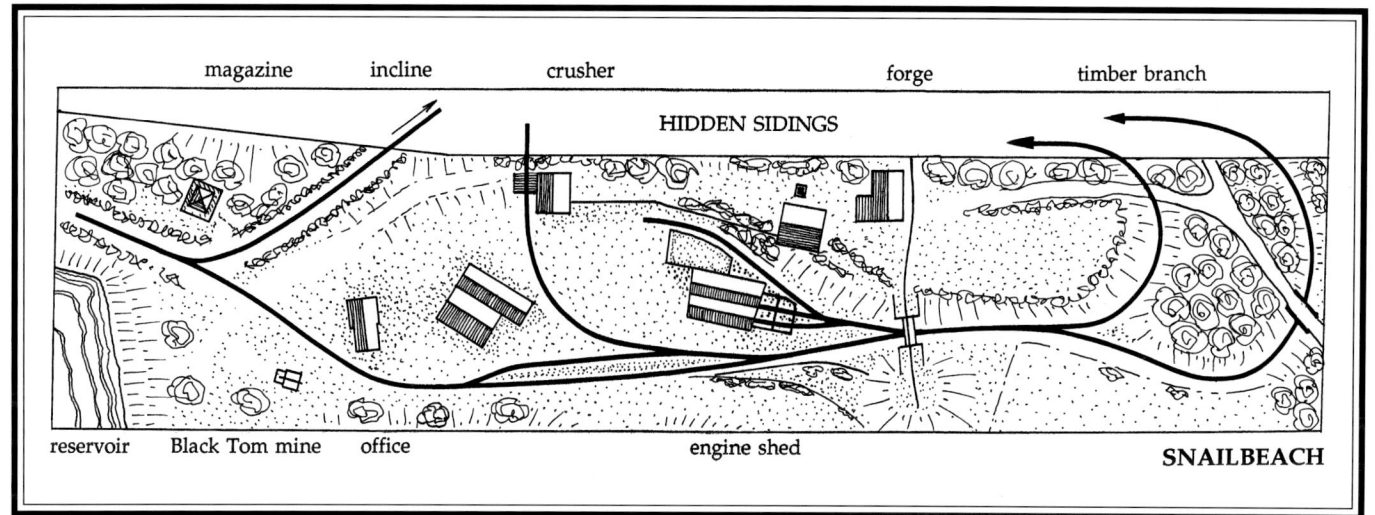

By the late 1920s, the SDR was operated by two Baldwins and the Kerr Stuart 0-4-2T. One of the former runs light through trees towards Snailbeach.

An Introduction to Modelling Narrow Gauge Railways

As built, the layout consisted of only the two baseboards on the right hand side of the accompanying drawing, but as more information became available, David decided to extend his model to include the terminus of the SDR and the short incline up which coal wagons were hauled to a power generating plant. Over the years, a lot of further research has been done, which has involved rebuilding some of the structures and constructing others which have long since been demolished, the details of which have only recently come to light.

The locos are all models of the prototypes which actually ran at some stage or other on the SDR. Fortunately, they were all available as kits from Gem and Chivers Finelines. The wagons they haul are also from kits, most, but by no means all of which are correct for a true scale model of the railway.

Llandydref (7n16.5)

Although Llandydref has been superseded on the exhibition circuit by the Gravetts' subsequent models (Ditchling Green and Abergynolwen), it is still an excellent example of a semi freelance layout and, moreover, one which is 7mm scale and which occupies a relatively small space.

The track plan is, like those of the other layouts featured in this section, quite simple, yet it is still capable of interesting operation. Representing the terminus of a Talyllyn-like slate carrier, the railway's works and the wharf where slate is transferred onto the standard gauge are included as well as

The Kerr Stuart Skylark class 0-4-2T on Snailbeach rounds the curve on the timber branch.

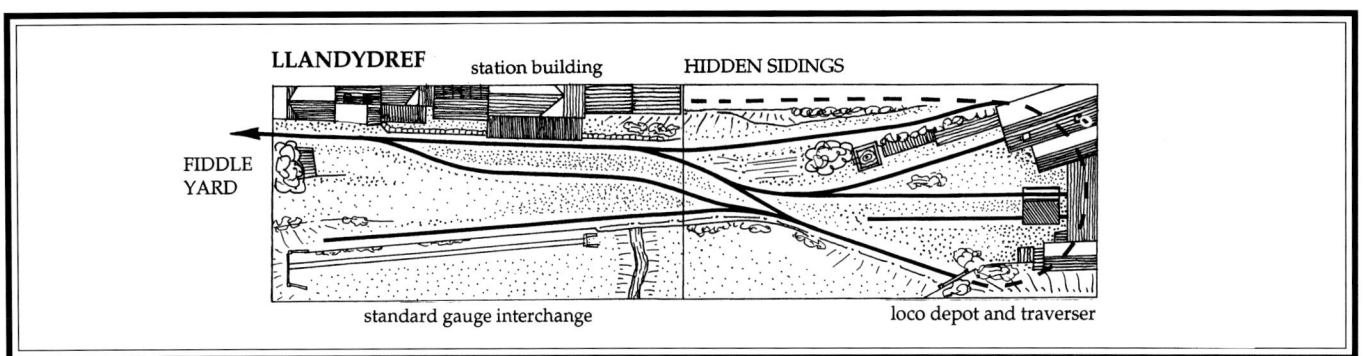

a station. In order to squeeze all this on to two baseboards (measuring 8 foot by 2 foot overall), a 9 inch radius curve, hidden from view, takes the main line round to the rear.

Trackwork is Peco, although when the layout was built, the only point available was a Y, so a number of 00 gauge 24 inch radius ones were used. The incorrect sleeper spacing and size were consequently hidden beneath weeds and ballast. The period modelled is that between the two world wars. Locos and stock are all weathered to varying degrees and look fairly run down, very evocative of a railway struggling to survive against increasing road competition and a falling demand for slate.

A passenger train behind 'Talyllyn' lurches over the points as it leaves Llandydref station. The loco is a Peco kit. (Gordon Gravett)

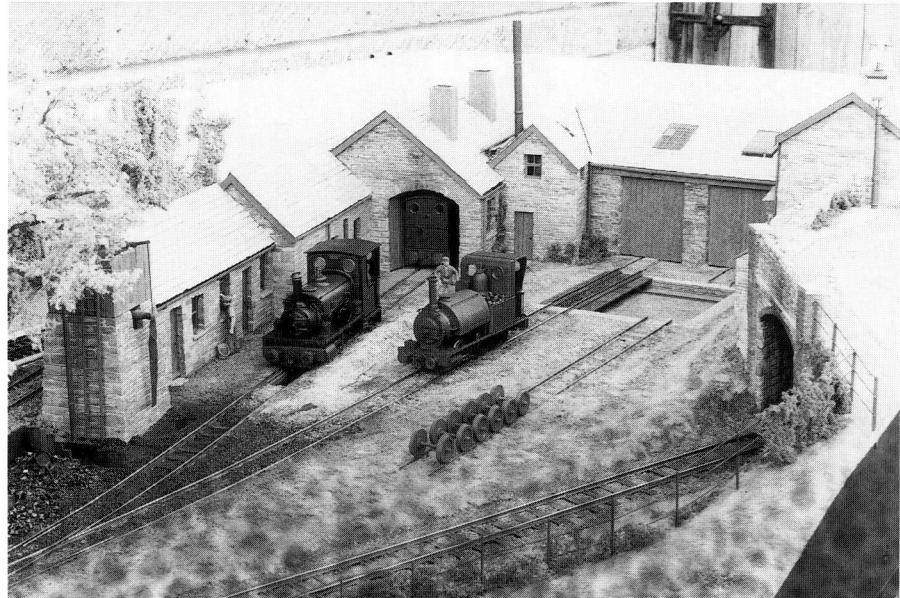

Right : The works at Llandydref. 'Talyllyn' is just moving off the traverser which provides access to other parts of the workshops. In the foreground can be seen the main line which disappears out of sight under the bridge and then turns round a 9 inch radius curve behind the works buildings.

Below : The cabless quarry loco is actually freelance and was kitbashed from a Hornby 'Desmond'.(Gordon Gravett)

Bottom : 'Talyllyn' and train at Llandydref. The coach is from a Wrightlines kit.(Gordon Gravett)

Chapter Nine
SOURCES OF INFORMATION

There can be no substitute for seeing the real thing and visiting preserved narrow gauge railways. The best known is probably the Talyllyn, here with No. 4 pushing the last train of the day out of Wharf station back to the carriage sheds at Pendre.

The Hampshire Narrow Gauge Railway was built by a group of enthusiasts in the garden of a private house, although it is now located in Southampton. Visits were by invitation only. A view of 'Wendy', a preserved Bagnall 0-4-0 saddle tank on the original site

Prototype

Most railway books these days fall into one of two categories: the photograph album covering many different lines and the detailed history of an individual company. Neither are very much use if you have no knowledge of narrow gauge railways at all, but there are two exceptions which are worth investing in for the newcomer. One is P B Whitehouse's and J B Snell's 'Narrow Gauge Railways Of The British Isles' published by David and Charles, which provides a well illustrated, readable and fairly comprehensive overview of railways in both the UK and Eire, although it does suffer from one or two minor inaccuracies. The other is James Boyd's 'Narrow Gauge Railways Of Mid Wales' published by the Oakwood Press. The latter is obviously more geographically restricted, but it does outline the histories of several of the better known lines including the Talyllyn, Welshpool and Llanfair and the Glyn Valley Tramway amongst others. More important for the modeller is that it includes drawings of locos and stock as well as plans of a number of stations.

There are some extremely well detailed histories of individual railways which you can obtain should you find one that particularly appeals to you. The publishers who specialise in narrow gauge titles are Plateway Press and the Oakwood Press, but most other railway publishers, such as Irwell, Ian Allan,

Other narrow gauge railways have been built as tourist attractions, often using the trackbeds of closed standard gauge lines. This is the 2 foot gauge Launceston Steam Railway. The loco is one of several small Hunslet saddle tanks purchased from a slate quarry.

Wild Swan, OPC and the Middleton Press have one or more titles of interest in their lists.

Books these days are expensive and it is worth remembering that your local library is free. If it hasn't got the title you want (or if it's out of print), they may be able to obtain it for you through the Inter Library Loan Scheme, though this does take time.

Videos, too, can often be very helpful, particularly as those dealing with narrow gauge subjects often include rare archive film of railways long since closed.

You might also consider joining the Narrow Gauge Railway Society or, if your interests are primarily in industrial lines, the Industrial Railway Society. Both publish magazines on a regular basis which contain articles of interest to modellers, whilst the former has a fairly extensive library from which modellers can borrow books and files by post. Contact addresses (at the time of writing: late 1995) are:

NGRS:
Mr P A Slater, 'Wayside', Stibb, Bude, Cornwall, EX23 9RG
IRS:
Mr B Mettam, 27 Glenfield Crescent, Newbold, Chesterfield, Derbyshire, S41 8SF

Finally, there is no substitute for seeing the real thing for yourself. There can be few people who are more than a couple of hour's drive or so from a narrow gauge railway, even if it is not one of the major preserved ones, such as the Festiniog or the Leighton Buzzard Railway, but a tourist line in the grounds of a stately home or a short enthusiasts' line on private ground. If you develop a fondness for one particular railway, it might be worth joining the preservation society if it has one, even if you don't want to work on it as a volunteer. Most societies have archival material in the form of documents, photos, drawings and the like which you should be able to gain access to.

Modelling

Most of the model railway magazines try to include the odd article on narrow gauge from time to time, but there is only one which specialises in the sub-

There are a number of exhibitions which are exclusively narrow gauge, the longest established one being EXPO-NG organised by the Greenwich & District Narrow Gauge Railway Society in Swanley in Kent. 'Llandydref' is typical of the many high quality layouts to be seen at such events.(Gordon Gravett)

An Introduction to Modelling Narrow Gauge Railways

ject. This is 'Narrow Gauge And Industrial Railway Modelling Review' (more commonly known as The Review!) which appears quarterly. You won't find it in Smiths or Menzies because it is only available on subscription from RAM Productions Ltd., P O Box 134, Pinner, Middlesex, HA5 3YN, although you might find it on sale at some exhibitions or in one or two model shops. It has features on the prototype as well as modelling and covers all scales from 16mm and below. Details of new products and reviews of kits are also included.

The two main modelling societies are the 009 Society and the 7mm Narrow Gauge Association. Each caters for followers of scales and gauges around 4mm and 7mm, so if you are interested in 4n12, for example, it is still worth joining the 009 Society. I have been a member of the former and am currently involved in the latter and would certainly recommend membership of one or the other. Both publish magazines which contain a great deal of information on the prototype and on modelling which the newcomer will find of use. Like Narrow Gauge and Industrial Railway Modelling Review, reviews and accounts of assembling kits also appear and are particularly useful as they often point out any pitfalls or problems in construction and, more importantly, how to overcome them. Additionally, each of the societies has produced a Handbook to serve as an introduction to their particular scale, with a great deal of practical information. Both also organise narrow gauge conventions and exhibitions from time to time and both have local area groups (the 009 Society more than the 7mm Narrow Gauge Association) where members can meet each other on a regular basis.

009 Society Membership Secretary
70 Grove Road, Shirley, Southampton, SO1 3EG

7mm Narrow Gauge Association
44 Longway Avenue, Cheltenham, GL53 9JJ.

Finally, there are also some exhibitions which are wholly narrow gauge. The oldest of these is organised by the Greenwich and District Narrow Gauge Railway Society and is known as **EXPO NARROW GAUGE** or **EXPO-NG** for short! This takes place in late October/early November and for the last few years, has been held at Swanley in Kent not far from London. There are also other specifically narrow gauge events, usually organised by local area groups of either the 009 Society or the 7mm Narrow Gauge Association throughout the country. If you can get to them, they are usually worth the effort as, apart from the layouts, specialist traders are also present who do not normally attend more conventional exhibitions. These events are all usually advertised in the model press.

Such events also enable visitors to see new kits and products and talk to their manufacturers who are usually in attendance. Backwoods Miniatures Vale of Rheidol loco rounding a curve on an exhibition layout.

There can be few people living more than a few hour's drive from a narrow gauge railway. This is the Leighton Buzzard Narrow Gauge Railway in Bedfordshire.

ACKNOWLEDGEMENTS

A book of this kind would be impossible without the help of many other narrow gauge modellers, whether it be supplying photographs and details of their models and layouts or allowing me or someone else to photograph them. The assistance of David Barham, Gordon Gravett, Barry Jeffery, and David Taylor (the Trade Liaison Officer of the 7mm Narrow Gauge Association) must be gratefully acknowledged, as must all those manufacturers and traders who loaned examples of their products. Roy C. Link also deserves thanks for providing a great deal of additional material. Of the members of the Greenwich & District Narrow Gauge Railway Society, David Gander must be mentioned for producing the drawings (and for taking photos of his layouts), whilst the aid of Miles Bevan, David Brewer, Richard Glover, Christopher Krupa, Neil Sayer and Peter Wilson has been invaluable. Finally this book is dedicated to **Imelda Mary Malin Cox** who arrived when the author had written about 24 pages and was six months old by the time it was completed.